DALLIANCE
and
UNDISCOVERED COUNTRY

DALLIANCE
and
UNDISCOVERED
COUNTRY

TOM STOPPARD

adapted from
ARTHUR SCHNITZLER

faber and faber
LONDON · BOSTON

First published in 1986
by Faber and Faber Limited
3 Queen Square London WC1N 3AU

Phototypeset by Wilmaset Birkenhead Wirral
Printed in Great Britain by
Richard Clay Ltd Bungay Suffolk
All rights reserved

British Library Cataloguing in Publication Data

Stoppard, Tom
Dalliance; and, Undiscovered country
I. Title   II. Stoppard, Tom. Undiscovered
country
822'.914   PR6069.T6

ISBN 0–571–14750–X
ISBN 0–571–14739–9 Pbk.

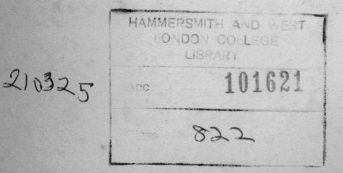

For Peter Wood

CONTENTS

INTRODUCTION

'An English version by . . .' Thus one has skirted the delicate
subject of a translation of Schnitzler by a writer with no
German. It is, admittedly, an odd business.

The problem is in the difference between theatre as text and
theatre as an event. Scholarship and playwrighting seldom go
hand in hand and this sad truth has given rise to an
arrangement, now commonplace, which is exemplified by the
process whereby *Das weite Land* became *Undiscovered Country*,
and *Liebelei* became *Dalliance*.

In the case of *Das weite Land*, the National Theatre provided
me with a literal transcript which aspired to be accurate and
readable rather than actable. I was also given the services of a
German linguist, John Harrison. Together – he with the German
text, I with the English – we went through the play line by line,
during which process small corrections were made and large
amounts of light were shed on the play I had before me. After
several weeks of splitting hairs with Harrison over alternatives
for innumerable words and phrases, the shadings of language
began to reveal themselves: carving one's way by this method
into the living rock is hardly likely to take one around the third
dimension, but as the relief becomes bolder so does the
translator until there is nothing to do but to begin.

However, this moment is the high-water mark of literal
accuracy. The first difference is that *Undiscovered Country* is
somewhat shorter than *Das weite Land*. The cuts were made
during rehearsals, partly for 'pace' and partly in compliance with
the director, Peter Wood, whose instinct was that the action
should break only once, at the end of Schnitzler's third act. As
for the other differences, they were often provoked by the sense
that in its original time and place the text gave a sharper account
of itself than it seemed to do on the page in faithful English in
1979. The temptation to add a flick here and there became

irresistible. So the text here published, though largely faithful to Schnitzler's play in word and, I trust, more so in spirit, departs from it sufficiently as to make one cautious about offering it as a 'translation': it is a record of what was performed at the National Theatre.

This disclaimer applies more forcibly to *Liebelei*, whose admirers will see that bolder liberties have been taken. The most obvious of these is that the third act of *Dalliance*, which in *Liebelei* has the same setting as the second act, has been removed to the wings and stage of the Josefstadt theatre and has been furnished with a tenor and a soprano, not to mention an off-stage orchestra, in mid-rehearsal. In stating that Wood had this idea before I got involved, I do so in the spirit of conceding the credit rather than passing the buck; I think it is a wonderful idea, allowing for a counterpoint between Christine's tragic love and the romanticized love-play of the operetta.

But the dialogue itself also underwent significant changes, the most notable being the last words of the play where Christine's denunciation of Theodore turns Schnitzler's view of Christine's last moments on its head. There are many other smaller alterations and additions, most of them designed to sharpen the dialogue and to tease more humour out of it. The implied hubris of this claim is not lost on me and, furthermore, a surprising number of critics turned out to be Schnitzler purists, who on their own evidence would have preferred *Liebelei* plain. I sympathize but apologies would be out of place.

T.S.
August 1986

to him, Genia! More than his profession, or his future, or me or his life. Oh God, I was so frightened about where it would lead to! And I kept silent. I had to keep silent. I had seen it coming, of course, from the day Otto entered this house. In all my resentment, my fear, my jealousy, I had to understand. You were so alone, Genia, and so much wronged . . . for so many years! And even if it hadn't been as good a man as Otto – I couldn't have blamed you. And now – now that he's gone, all my resentment and jealousy have gone too, and I only ask myself: how will she bear it? She – who loved him!

GENIA: Mrs von Aigner, I truly am not worth such sympathy. I will try to forget him. And I will succeed. That is certain – as certain as that he will succeed too. You mustn't worry. There was no understanding between us. I promise you . . . We're not even going to write to each other. You may count on that.

MRS VON AIGNER: You're so good, Genia!

GENIA: I'm merely practical, Mrs von Aigner, only . . . practical.

MRS VON AIGNER: Can't you find any other name for me? I'm his mother.

GENIA: No, no, no, I can't! ·
(*She breaks down.*)

MRS VON AIGNER: Genia, Genia. Don't cry, Genia!
(*She strokes* GENIA's *hair.*)
Child, child – do calm yourself. You can see, of course, that my choice is made . . . I cannot hate you. We will bear his absence together. We're going to be friends, Genia. It's all we can be.
(FRIEDRICH *enters from the veranda. A dark greatcoat over his black frockcoat. Quickly buttons his greatcoat, composes his expression.* GENIA *stares at him inquiringly.* FRIEDRICH *gives a fixed smile, without nodding. He speaks to* MRS VON AIGNER *in his laughing mischievous vein, which is now mask-like.*)

FRIEDRICH: How do you do, madam.

(*He takes her proffered hand with only the faintest show of hesitation.*)

How are you?

MRS VON AIGNER: Well. Back so early from town?

FRIEDRICH: From town? No. I'm just going there now. I've just been for my morning stroll. A . . . glorious day . . .

MRS VON AIGNER: You've had a nice trip?

FRIEDRICH: Yes, very nice. Very nice. No complaints. Good weather, interesting people, what more could one want?

MRS VON AIGNER: Oh yes, I have to send someone's regards to you.

FRIEDRICH: Regards? To me?

MRS VON AIGNER: You'll be somewhat surprised. Regards from Dr von Aigner.

FRIEDRICH: From your husband?

MRS VON AIGNER: Yes, early this morning. Before I left the house there was a letter from him, the first for many years. And in a few days he's coming in person. A conference with the Minister, so he writes.

FRIEDRICH: He'll be Minister himself one day, your husband. Altogether a remarkable chap, a most remarkable man. He still has a great future.

MRS VON AIGNER: Do you really think so?

FRIEDRICH: Why not?

MRS VON AIGNER: Well, he also mentions his poor health . . .

FRIEDRICH: Poor health! . . . He'll outlive us all. Forgive me, naturally I can, of course, only speak for myself, that's all anyone can do . . . (*Laughs.*) A very interesting chap . . . we talked a lot together . . . in those few days . . . I like him.

MRS VON AIGNER: And he seems to have taken you very much to his heart. Yes, it's a strange letter. Almost touching. And a little affected. But it's too late for him to change now.

FRIEDRICH: Much too late.

MRS VON AIGNER: Well, goodbye for now.

FRIEDRICH: Goodbye, ma'am. And when your husband

comes here our house is naturally . . . *Les amis de nos amis* . . . and so forth. Adieu, madam.

MRS VON AIGNER: (*As* GENIA *accompanies her for a few steps*) Goodbye, dear Mrs Hofreiter.

(*She leaves and* GENIA *returns quickly.* FRIEDRICH *is standing motionless.*)

GENIA: Well? . . . Everything . . . all right – ?

FRIEDRICH: (*Looking at her*) Well. . . !

GENIA: He's wounded?! Friedrich! . . .

FRIEDRICH: He's dead!

GENIA: Friedrich, Friedrich . . .

(*She goes to him and seizes him by the shoulders.*)

You shook hands with his mother.

FRIEDRICH: (*Shrugs.*) I didn't know that she . . . would be with you. What was I supposed to do?

GENIA: Dead . . . dead! . . . (*Suddenly, at him*) Murderer!

FRIEDRICH: It was a duel. I'm no murderer.

GENIA: Why, why . . . ?

FRIEDRICH: Why? – Obviously . . . because I felt like it.

GENIA: That's just not true! Don't make yourself out worse than you are. You didn't want to do it. It was a terrible accident . . . You didn't want to . . . It isn't true . . .

FRIEDRICH: At the moment he stood facing me, it was true.

GENIA: You didn't even hate him and yet you killed him – You vain, contemptible monster. . . !

FRIEDRICH: It isn't as simple as . . . You can't look into my soul. No one can. I'm sorry for poor Mrs von Aigner. And for poor old Mr von Aigner, too. But I can't help them. Nor you. Nor help him. Nor me. It had to be so.

GENIA: Had to? –

FRIEDRICH: When he stood facing me, with the insolence of youth in his eyes, I knew then . . . it was him or me.

GENIA: You're lying, he wouldn't have . . . he wouldn't . . .

FRIEDRICH: You're wrong. He wanted it, as I did. It was life or death. Him . . . or me . . .

(ERNA *and* MAUER *enter from the garden.* ERNA *remains*

145

standing at the door. MAUER *goes quickly to* GENIA, *and presses her hand.*)

Ah, Mauer, you here already?

MAUER: There was nothing more for me to do.

GENIA: Where is his body?

MAUER: On its way.

GENIA: Where to?

MAUER: His mother's house.

GENIA: Does she know . . . who will tell her. . . ?

MAUER: No one has dared to yet.

GENIA: I will tell her. It's my duty. I'm going to her.

FRIEDRICH: Genia . . . just a moment. When you come back, I probably won't be here. I can't ask you to give me your hand, but – are we just going to say farewell?

GENIA: (*Remembering*) Joey's coming. Any time now.

FRIEDRICH: Joey? I'll wait for him . . . Then . . .

GENIA: What are you going to do?

FRIEDRICH: Go to town. Give myself up. Nothing will happen to me anyway. I have only defended my honour. Perhaps I'll get bail and they'll let me . . . though of course they might suspect me of fleeing the country . . .

GENIA: You can think of that!! And he's lying dead.

FRIEDRICH: Yes, I can. He's got it easier now. For him it's all over. But for me – I'm still in this world. And I intend to go on living in it . . . Please make up your mind. Which way is it going to be?

GENIA: (*Staring at him*) It's over. (*About to go*) It's finished.

MAUER: Frau Genia . . . You can't walk that road alone. Allow me to go with you.

(MAUER *and* GENIA *leave.* ERNA *at the door is motionless.* FRIEDRICH *stands stiffly as before.*)

ERNA: What will you do?

FRIEDRICH: I'll leave the district of course . . . clear out altogether.

ERNA: Wherever you want to go, Friedrich – I will follow you.

FRIEDRICH: Declined, with thanks.

ERNA: I know it more surely than ever, Friedrich, we belong together.

FRIEDRICH: You are mistaken. At the moment you are under the spell of these events. Perhaps you're even impressed that I . . . but that's an illusion. It's all illusion. I'll fold up like a pocket knife, soon enough. It's over, Erna, for us as well. You're twenty years old, and you don't belong to me.

ERNA: (*Still where she was*) You are younger than any of them.

FRIEDRICH: Hush! I know what youth is. It's not an hour since I saw it. It glows, it laughs, it has an insolence in its eye. I know what youth is. And I can't shoot them all . . . Stay where you are, have as good a time as you can . . .

ERNA: (*Listening*) A car.

FRIEDRICH: (*Still motionless*) Joey.

ERNA: (*Now a little nearer to him*) Believe me, Friedrich, I love you, I belong to you.

FRIEDRICH: I belong to no one on this earth. No one. Nor do I wish to . . .

A BOY'S VOICE: (*In the garden*) Mother! Father!

FRIEDRICH: (*Moans quietly, once.*) Joey, I'm coming. Here I am. (*He walks quickly out on to the veranda.* ERNA *remains standing.*)

DALLIANCE
Liebelei
by Arthur Schnitzler

In an English version by
TOM STOPPARD

CHARACTERS

FRITZ

THEODORE

MIZI

CHRISTINE

A GENTLEMAN

FRAU BINDER

HERR WEIRING

A TENOR

A SOPRANO

FRITZ'S MANSERVANT

STAGE MANAGER

In addition, at the operetta:
    Conductor
    Musicians
    Stage-hands

The play takes place in Vienna in the 1890s.

Dalliance was first performed at the Lyttelton Theatre, London, on 27 May 1986. The cast was as follows:

FRITZ	Stephen Moore
THEODORE	Tim Curry
MIZI	Sally Dexter
CHRISTINE	Brenda Blethyn
A GENTLEMAN	Basil Henson
FRAU BINDER	Sara Kestelman
HERR WEIRING	Michael Bryant
A TENOR	Neil Daglish
A SOPRANO	Roz Clifton
FRITZ'S MANSERVANT	Alan Haywood
STAGE MANAGER	Saul Reichlin
ORCHESTRA MANAGER	Steven Law
Directed by	Peter Wood
Designed by	Carl Toms

ACT ONE

The reception room of Fritz's flat.
There is a table to eat at, and a sideboard, etc. There is a piano.
There is a divan. French doors at the back give on to a terrace or
garden partly visible to us. There are doors to a kitchen and to a
lobby leading to the street.
FRITZ *is discovered practising marksmanship with a duelling pistol.*
The MANSERVANT *is on hand to bring the paper target back to*
FRITZ *for his inspection, and to reload the pistol while* FRITZ *takes*
a second shot with the second of the pair of pistols. FRITZ *aims and*
fires for the second time. The MANSERVANT *brings the target for the*
second time. It is clear from the way FRITZ *inspects the target that he*
is not much of a shot. There does not appear to be a hole in the target
at all. Before FRITZ *shoots again, he steps forward for a shorter*
range, then shoots.
THEODORE *enters the room from the lobby. He is wearing a coat or*
cloak. He sees FRITZ *and calls to him.*

THEODORE: Fritz!
    (FRITZ *turns to him, holding the gun.*)
    Don't shoot!
FRITZ: I don't.
THEODORE: What exactly. . . ?
FRITZ: Sport. And what. . . ?
THEODORE: Supper.
FRITZ: I'm afraid I . . .
THEODORE: It's all arranged.
FRITZ: All right. Where are we going? Did you keep the cab?
THEODORE: No.
    (THEODORE *takes off his overcoat and throws it down over a*
    chair.)
FRITZ: Well . . . why don't you take your coat off?
    (*Meanwhile the* MANSERVANT *has put both pistols into a*

5

*wooden pistol case. Two or three paper targets remain on the
ground outside the French windows. The* MANSERVANT *leaves
through the kitchen doors, closing them behind him after saying,
'Goodnight, sir' and being ignored. Meanwhile* FRITZ *spots
two or three letters, newly arrived, which have been placed on
his desk. He seizes the letters anxiously and sifts through them
rapidly.*)

Ah – the post!

THEODORE: Love letters? I say, you are in a state. Is this the
post-coital one hears so much about?

(*Whatever* FRITZ *might have been expecting is not there. He
starts to open the letters.*)

I always say one should never put it in writing.

FRITZ: Nothing. One from Lensky . . . and my father . . .

THEODORE: Don't mind me. What has your father got to say?

FRITZ: Not much . . . wants me to go down to the country for a
week at Whitsun.

THEODORE: Very good idea. Six months would be even better.
Fresh air, fresh pastures, milkmaids . . .

FRITZ: It isn't a dairy farm.

THEODORE: Even so.

FRITZ: Do you want to come?

THEODORE: 'Fraid I can't.

FRITZ: Why not?

THEODORE: God, I've got my anatomy viva, again! – I'd only go
to make sure you stayed there.

FRITZ: Oh, come off it, I'm all right.

THEODORE: What you need is a change of scene. Really. It was
quite apparent the other when-was-it – as soon as you got
out into the country on a bright spring day you became
quite tolerable.

FRITZ: Thanks very much.

THEODORE: Now it's wearing off again. We're back in the
danger zone. No, really, you've no idea how it improved
you, getting away from all this, you were really quite
sensible. Like old times. Even since then when we went out

6

with those two popsies you were good fun. But all that's
over, now that you can't stop thinking of 'that woman'.
(FRITZ *makes an impatient gesture*.)
If you think I'll let you ruin my life over a woman you're
very much mistaken.

FRITZ: My God, you do go on.

THEODORE: Fritz, I'm not asking you to give her up. I just
want you to treat it as a normal affair instead of this grand
opera which'll be the finish of you. Love is for operettas.
Honestly, if you could get out of her spell you'd be amazed
how much better the two of you would get on. You'd see
that there's nothing *fatale* about the *femme*, she's just
another pretty wife put into the world to brighten up your
day, just like any other woman who is reasonably young
and decent-looking and gets about a bit.

FRITZ: What do you mean, the finish of me?

THEODORE: I mean exactly that. I'm terrified you're going to
run off with her one day.

FRITZ: Oh, that.

THEODORE: Not only that.

FRITZ: That's right, Theo, not only that.

THEODORE: Just don't do anything silly.

FRITZ: It's not up to me.

THEODORE: What isn't?

FRITZ: Nothing. She's been wrong before.

THEODORE: How? What are you talking about?

FRITZ: She's been on edge lately . . . well, on and off.

THEODORE: Why?

FRITZ: No reason at all. Nerves. (*Smiles*.) A guilty conscience if
you like.

THEODORE: You said – she'd been wrong before. . . ?

FRITZ: Yes. Only today . . .

THEODORE: What happened today?

FRITZ: She thinks we're being watched.

THEODORE: Watched?

FRITZ: She's seeing things, that's all. Literally. Hallucinations.

She looks through this gap in the curtains and she sees
someone or other standing out there on the street corner
and she's convinced – I mean, is it possible to make out a
face at this distance?

THEODORE: Hardly.

FRITZ: Exactly, that's what I tell her. But then it's awful – she's
terrified to set foot outside. She gets quite hysterical and
bursts into tears and says she wants to die with me.

THEODORE: Naturally.

FRITZ: Today she made me go outside to have a look round, as
if I just happened to be stepping out of doors. Needless to
say there was no one I knew for miles around. So that
disposes of that, wouldn't you say? Wouldn't you say,
Theo? People don't just disappear into thin air. Theo?

THEODORE: What do you want me to say? All right, people
don't disappear into thin air, sometimes they hide in
doorways.

FRITZ: I looked in every one.

THEODORE: You must have been the picture of innocence.

FRITZ: There was nobody. As I said – hallucinations.

THEODORE: Absolutely. Only let it be a lesson to you to be
more careful.

FRITZ: He can't suspect anything. I would have noticed. I
actually had supper with them after the theatre yesterday.
They invited me to their musical evening tomorrow, him
and her. It was all so ridiculously hail-fellow-well-m– –
maybe that means he knows.

THEODORE: Listen, Fritz – do me a favour – all right, I *am*
asking you to give her up. If only for *my* sake. Think of *my*
nerves. Now, I know it's absolutely against your nature and
your principles to end an affair before you've begun another
one, so I've been smoothing the sheets, way, rather.

FRITZ: Oh, have you?

THEODORE: You haven't noticed? After I took you on my date
with Mizi, and got her to bring along her best friend? And
do you deny you took quite a fancy to the little darling?

8

FRITZ: She was rather sweet actually . . . yes, awfully sweet. And you can't imagine how I long for a little simple affection without all the drama . . . for someone soothing to stand by me when life gets fraught.

THEODORE: That's it exactly. The warrior's rest. That's what they're for. Convalescence. That's why I've always been against these so-called fascinating women. Women have no business to be fascinating, their job is to be pleasant. You must find your happiness in pastures where I look for mine, where there are no dramas and no dangers, no grand opera, easy in and easy out from first kiss to fond parting.

FRITZ: Yes, that's right.

THEODORE: After all, women are perfectly happy being women, so why do we keep trying to turn them into angels and demons, it's so unhealthy.

FRITZ: Yes, she really was an angel, Mizi's friend . . .

THEODORE: You're doing it again.

FRITZ: No – no –

THEODORE: You're hopeless –

FRITZ: No, I'm with you – convalescence, lie them down in fresh pastures, whatever you say.

THEODORE: Otherwise I withdraw my support. I've had enough of your romantic tragedies. I'm bored with them. And if you feel compelled to demonstrate your famous conscience, I'll tell you my simple philosophy in these matters: better me than somebody else; and there is *always* somebody else. (*The doorbell rings.*)

FRITZ: (*Startled*) Who can that be?

THEODORE: Well, go and see. Oh God, he's gone white as a sheet – calm down this minute. It's the popsies.

FRITZ: (*Relieved*) What?

THEODORE: I took the liberty of inviting them round.

FRITZ: But why didn't you say so? My man will have gone.

THEODORE: We will have to do.

(FRITZ *goes out to the front door.*)

FRITZ: (*Outside*) Good evening, Mizi.

9

(MIZI *enters carrying a parcel, followed by* FRITZ.)
Where's Christine?

MIZI: She's coming on later. How are you, Dory? I hope you don't mind, Fritz, but Theodore asked us.

FRITZ: Delighted. The only thing he forgot was –

THEODORE: He forgot nothing. (*To* MIZI) Did you bring everything I wrote down for you?

MIZI: Of course. Where should I put it?

FRITZ: Let me take it. It can go on the sideboard for the moment.

MIZI: I brought something extra which wasn't on your list.

THEODORE: What is it?

MIZI: Chocolate éclairs.

THEODORE: You shall have your cake.

FRITZ: Let me have your hat, Mizi – that's right. So, why didn't Christine come with you?

MIZI: She was taking her father down to the theatre, then she's catching the tram back here.

THEODORE: What a good girl.

MIZI: Well, her father's been a bit down in the dumps since the old lady died.

FRITZ: Christine's mother?

MIZI: No, her auntie who was living with them. She never knew her mother.

THEODORE: Christine's father – little man with long, grey hair?

MIZI: No, he's got short hair.

FRITZ: How would you know him?

THEODORE: I was watching the show at the Josefstadt with Lensky the other day and I had a good look at the chap playing the double-bass –

MIZI: It's not a double-bass, it's a violin.

THEODORE: Well, I said he was small.

MIZI: (*To* FRITZ) You've got a nice place here, *très élégant, monsieur*, really lovely. What's the view?

FRITZ: This window, *ma'm'selle*, looks out on the Stroghgasse. Next door –

THEODORE: What's all this coyness? I want us to be on familiar
   terms, not to say intimate.

MIZI: Eat first.

THEODORE: A very middle-class idea. Still, I suppose it's
   reassuring. And how is your mother, if I may be so
   familiar?

MIZI: Would you believe – ?

THEODORE: I would. Toothache. She's always got toothache.
   You must tell her about dentists.

MIZI: The doctor says it's her age.

THEODORE: It is, it is. Everything is our age. Our age is the
   toothache age, rotten to the teeth.

   (MIZI *picks up a photograph frame.*)

MIZI: Who's this?

THEODORE: It doesn't show in the photographs.

MIZI: (*To* FRITZ) Goodness, it's you, in uniform. Were you in
   the army?

FRITZ: Yes.

MIZI: A Dragoon! Yellow or black?

FRITZ: The Yellows.

MIZI: A Yellow Dragoon!

THEODORE: She's gone. Mizi, wake up!

MIZI: So now you're in the Reserve?

FRITZ: That's right.

MIZI: I bet you look like something in your breeches.

THEODORE: You seem to know a lot about it. Listen, Mizi, I'm
   an officer too.

MIZI: A Dragoon?

THEODORE: Yes.

MIZI: Why ever didn't you say?

THEODORE: I wanted to be loved for myself.

MIZI: Well, next time we go out anywhere together you must
   wear your uniform.

THEODORE: I only put it on for funerals. But I'll be wearing it
   for August – I've got manoeuvres.

MIZI: Heavens, it won't wait till August.

THEODORE: No, that's true – our love is eternal, of course, but there is a limit.

MIZI: Who thinks about August in May? Isn't that right, Fritz? Why did you stand us up last night?

FRITZ: Where?

MIZI: After the theatre, of course.

FRITZ: Didn't Theo make my excuses?

THEODORE: Of course I did.

MIZI: Excuses are no use to me. I mean to Christine. A promise is a promise.

FRITZ: I honestly would have much rather been with you.

MIZI: Honestly?

FRITZ: But I couldn't. I was sharing a box with a couple of friends, and I couldn't tear myself away.

MIZI: You couldn't tear yourself away all right – who was the lovely lady? Did you think we couldn't see you through the peephole?

FRITZ: From behind the curtain?

MIZI: You sat right to the back of the box.

FRITZ: I find it helps if you can't see the actors.

MIZI: You were sitting behind her, the one in the black velvet dress, and you kept leaning forward like this.

FRITZ: I see you *were* keeping an eye on me.

MIZI: Well, it's none of my affair. But if I were in Christine's shoes . . . How is it that Theo is always free after the theatre – why doesn't *he* have to have supper with a couple of friends?

THEODORE: (*Meaningfully*) Yes, why don't *I* have to have supper with a couple of friends?

(*The doorbell rings.*)

MIZI: That'll be Christine.

(FRITZ *goes out.*)

THEODORE: Mizi, you can do me a favour. Forget your military career, at least for the moment.

MIZI: What can you mean?

THEODORE: You didn't learn how a Hussar dresses from the army manual.

(FRITZ *and* CHRISTINE *enter,* CHRISTINE *carrying a bunch of roses.*)

CHRISTINE: Hello . . . (*To* FRITZ) Did you mind us coming? You're not cross?

FRITZ: My dear girl, Theodore is occasionally the one with a good idea.

THEODORE: Well, is your father fiddling away?

CHRISTINE: He certainly is. I took him all the way to the Josefstadt.

FRITZ: So Mizi said. What have you got there?

CHRISTINE: I've brought you some flowers.

FRITZ: You're an angel – Isn't she an absolute – (*catching* THEO's *eye*) – darling! – Wait, let's put them in the vase there.

THEODORE: No, no, you have absolutely no sense of style. Flowers should be scattered carelessly over the table. Except that it should be after the table is laid. Ideally they should fall from the ceiling but I suppose we can't manage that.

FRITZ: Hardly.

THEODORE: I know! – let's put them in the vase over there! (*He puts them in a vase.*)

MIZI: It's getting dark, boys and girls, we'll light the lamp in a moment.

THEODORE: Lamp? Ridiculous idea! We'll light candles! That'll be much prettier. Come on, Mizi, you can give me a hand. (*There are two silver candelabra, lacking candles, which* THEODORE *picks up and takes out into the kitchen, ushering* MIZI *out with him.*)

FRITZ: How are you, my pet?

CHRISTINE: I'm all right now.

FRITZ: Only now?

CHRISTINE: I've missed you so much.

FRITZ: You saw me yesterday.

CHRISTINE: Saw you?

FRITZ: Through the peephole, Mizi said.

CHRISTINE: Don't be unkind.

FRITZ: You're such a baby. I couldn't get away. You could see that.

CHRISTINE: Yes . . . but, Fritz – who were the people in the box?

FRITZ: Friends – what do their names matter?

CHRISTINE: And the woman in black?

FRITZ: Oh, my dear girl, I can never remember clothes.

CHRISTINE: Oh, really!

FRITZ: Or rather, only in special cases. For instance that dark grey blouse you wore the first time I saw you . . . oh – and your pendant – I recognize that too!

CHRISTINE: So when did I wear it?

FRITZ: It was . . . well, some time ago, that day we went for a walk in the gardens along by the railway and we watched all those children playing . . . wasn't it?

CHRISTINE: Yes. So you do think of me now and then.

FRITZ: All the time, my sweet.

CHRISTINE: I think of you all the time, too, Fritz – every minute – I'm only happy when I can see you.

FRITZ: We see each other all the time.

CHRISTINE: All the time?!

FRITZ: Well, so to speak. Come the summer it will be less. What would you say if I went away for a few weeks?

CHRISTINE: What . . . ? You're going away?

FRITZ: No, but suppose I want to be on my own for a week.

CHRISTINE: Whatever for?

FRITZ: I'm only saying suppose – I know what I'm like and sometimes I'm like that. Besides, you might not want to see *me* for a few days. I'd understand.

CHRISTINE: I'll never feel like that, Fritz.

FRITZ: You can't be sure.

CHRISTINE: I am sure. I love you.

FRITZ: And I . . . you.

CHRISTINE: You're everything to me, Fritz – I'd do anything, I can't imagine a time when I wouldn't want to see you, for ever and ever.

FRITZ: Dear girl, don't say that – ever and ever makes me ever so nervous. Don't let's speak of eternity.

CHRISTINE: Oh, don't worry, Fritz – I know it's not really for ever.

FRITZ: I didn't mean that. Perhaps it'll happen that we can't live without each other – but we can't know . . . people can't.

(THEODORE *and* MIZI *now enter from the kitchen holding the blazing candles.*)

THEODORE: Now, will you look at that! Isn't that nicer than some silly lamp?

FRITZ: You're a born romantic, Theo.

THEODORE: I know. Well, children, what do you think about supper?

MIZI: Yes – come on, Christine!

FRITZ: Hang on, I'll show you where everything is.

MIZI: The first thing we need is a tablecloth.

(THEODORE *produces one with a flourish from behind his back or from his sleeve.*)

THEODORE: (*With an accent*) First – ze cloth de table – I 'ave ze very thing – in fact I 'ave ze veritable cloth – ze true cloth – accept no substitutes –

MIZI: (*Laughing*) He should be in the music-halls. Dory, when are you going to take me to the Orpheum? You said you would. But Christine has to come too, and Lieutenant Fritz – and then *we'll* be the friends in his box.

FRITZ: Yes . . . oh yes.

MIZI: And the lady in black can go home alone.

FRITZ: It's really too silly the way you go on about her.

MIZI: Oh she's nothing to us . . . Now – cutlery? – good – and plates. . . ?

FRITZ: Plates! – in the plate cupboard.

MIZI: Fine, thank you, we can manage without you now – leave it to us, you'll only be in the way. (*To* CHRISTINE) Have you seen the photo of Fritz in uniform?

CHRISTINE: No.

MIZI: You should see it – it's devastating.

(MIZI *goes into the kitchen.* CHRISTINE *picks up the
photograph, looks at it long and lovingly and eventually
replaces it. She notices the men looking bemusedly at her.
Embarrassed, she hurries into the kitchen after* MIZI.)

THEODORE: You don't mind, do you? I love evenings like this.

FRITZ: Yes, they're very nice.

THEODORE: I feel so at peace, don't you? This is the life, isn't
it?

FRITZ: Well, it's one of them.

MIZI: (*Off*) I say, Fritz – is there any coffee in the machine?

FRITZ: Yes, but you could make coffee on the primus, the
machine takes ages.

THEODORE: I'll give you a dozen so-called fascinating women
for one unspoiled little popsie.

FRITZ: They're not to be spoken of in the same breath.

THEODORE: Absolutely. The trouble with real women is that we
can't stand the ones who want us, and we're mad about the
ones we can't have.

(MIZI *and* CHRISTINE *enter with things for the table. They
begin to set out the tableware and the food.*)

MIZI: What's all that? We want to be let in on it.

THEODORE: Nothing for your ears, little girls. We're
philosophizing. (*To* FRITZ) If this was our last evening with
these two it wouldn't be any different, would it?

FRITZ: Our last evening together . . . well, I don't know . . .
partings are always a bit sad, even the ones we put in our
diaries.

CHRISTINE: Fritz, where's the cruet?

FRITZ: The cruet?

CHRISTINE: Condiments?

FRITZ: Condiments! Salt, pepper, oil and vinegar! – in the
condiment cupboard!

THEODORE: (*To* MIZI) Come here, minx.

(FRITZ *helps* CHRISTINE. MIZI *comes to* THEODORE.
THEODORE *sprawls on the divan and* MIZI *joins him there.*)

CHRISTINE: You've got life organized, haven't you?

FRITZ: Yes, haven't I?

CHRISTINE: Fritz – won't you tell me?

FRITZ: What?

CHRISTINE: Who the lady was.

FRITZ: Who was that lady I saw you with last night? No – don't make me cross. Remember what we said. No questions. That's what's so nice about being with you. Nothing else exists. I don't ask you things.

CHRISTINE: You can ask me anything.

FRITZ: (*Sharply*) But I don't. I don't want to know anything. (*There is an awkward silence.* MIZI *hurries over to* CHRISTINE.)

MIZI: Goodness, what a mess you're making of that . . . (*She takes things out of* FRITZ's *hands and arranges the table accordingly.*) There we are . . .

THEODORE: I say, Fritz, is there anything to drink?

FRITZ: Oh, yes, I'm sure there's something. (FRITZ *finds a couple of bottles in the sideboard.* THEODORE *surveys the table.*)

THEODORE: Excellent.

MIZI: I think that's everything.

FRITZ: Here we are.

THEODORE: What about the roses falling from the ceiling?

MIZI: Yes, quite right – we forgot the roses. (MIZI *takes the flowers out of the vase, stands on a chair and scatters the roses on the table.*) There you are!

THEODORE: Careful! – not on the plates.

CHRISTINE: Honestly, she's quite out of hand . . .

FRITZ: Where would you like to sit, Christine?

THEODORE: Where's the corkscrew?

FRITZ: In the corkscrew drawer.

THEODORE: Let's eat first and afterwards Fritz will play for us. What do you say?

MIZI: Oh yes, that would be devastating!

FRITZ: (*To* CHRISTINE) Shall I?

CHRISTINE: Oh, please! I've been wanting you to for ages.

FRITZ: You play a bit, don't you?

CHRISTINE: Oh, heavens . . .

MIZI: She plays beautifully – and she can sing.

FRITZ: Really? You never told me.

CHRISTINE: When did you ask?

FRITZ: Wherever did you learn to sing?

CHRISTINE: I didn't learn exactly. Father taught me a bit but I haven't got much of a voice. And there hasn't been a lot of singing in the house since my auntie died.

FRITZ: What do you do with yourself all day?

CHRISTINE: Heavens, I've got lots to do.

FRITZ: Housework, you mean?

CHRISTINE: And I copy out scores.

FRITZ: Music scores?

CHRISTINE: Yes, of course.

THEODORE: That must be tremendously well paid.
  (*The others laugh.*)
  Well, I'd pay tremendously well for it. Copying music sounds like a frightful chore.

MIZI: And she's silly to punish herself. (*To* CHRISTINE) If I had your voice I'd have gone on stage years ago.

THEODORE: You don't need a voice. And I suppose you do nothing all day, being in the theatre.

MIZI: I beg your pardon – a seamstress is the busiest person in the Josefstadt.

THEODORE: 'Seams, madam? I know not seams.'

MIZI: (*Puzzled, cross*) Are you making fun of me?

FRITZ: (*To* CHRISTINE) You must sing something for us.

THEODORE: What will you have, Mizi? And before you say anything the cakes come last. First you have to eat some proper food.

FRITZ: And drink several glasses of wine, starting with this one.
  (FRITZ *starts to pour out the wine.*)

THEODORE: Not like that. That's not how it's done nowadays. Don't you keep up with society?
(THEODORE *takes the bottle and pours the wine with considerable pomp, naming it and proclaiming the vintage in a manner which, however, makes the precise year unintelligible.*)
Xeres de la Frontera, mil huit cent cinquante . . .
(*He repeats the procedure for each glass and then sits down.*)

MIZI: He's such a fool.

THEODORE: Cheers!

MIZI: Your health, Theodore.

THEODORE: (*Standing*) Ladies and gentlemen –

FRITZ: Not yet!

THEODORE: (*Sitting down*) Right!
(*They start to eat.*)

MIZI: I love people who make speeches at the table.

THEODORE: All of them?

MIZI: I've got a cousin who does them in rhyming couplets.

THEODORE: What regiment is he in?

MIZI: Oh, do stop it. He recites poetry – he's devastating, Christine, and not as immature as some people either.

THEODORE: Well, it's not uncommon for elderly folk to speak in rhyme.

FRITZ: You're not drinking, Christine.

THEODORE: Here's to old soldiers, may they live to recite again.

MIZI: And to young lieutenants who hardly speak at all, like Fritz. Fritz – we'll drink a friendship cup if you like – and Christine must do the same with Theodore.

THEODORE: But not in this wine – this is no wine for our cups.
(*He takes up the other bottle and goes through the same procedure as before.*)
Voslauer Auslese . . . You'll find this an affectionate little cup, with just a hint of promiscuity.

MIZI: (*Sipping the wine*) Ah!

THEODORE: Can't you wait till we've all got a glass? All right, my friends, before we pledge let's drink to fortune and that happy chance which – which has brought the four of us . . . and the rest of it.

MIZI: That'll do.

(FRITZ *links arms with* MIZI, THEODORE *with* CHRISTINE, *all with glasses in their hands, as they drink.* FRITZ *kisses* MIZI. THEODORE *tries to kiss* CHRISTINE.)

CHRISTINE: (*Smiling*) Oh, are we supposed to?

THEODORE: Certainly, otherwise it doesn't count.

(*He kisses* CHRISTINE.)

MIZI: It's awfully hot in here.

FRITZ: That's because of all those candles.

MIZI: And the wine.

(THEODORE *picks up an éclair for* MIZI.)

THEODORE: Here you are, this is what you get for being a good girl.

(*He puts the éclair in her mouth.*)

There . . . good?

MIZI: Very!

THEODORE: Well, bad girls get two. Come on, Fritz – now's the moment. Play us something.

FRITZ: Do you want me to, Christine?

CHRISTINE: Oh, please!

MIZI: Play something devastating.

(THEODORE *fills the glasses.*)

(*Drinking*) No more for me.

CHRISTINE: The wine's so heavy.

THEODORE: Fritz!

MIZI: Lieutenant Fritz – play 'The False Hussar'.

FRITZ: 'The False Hussar' – how does it go?

MIZI: Dory, can't you play 'The False Hussar'?

THEODORE: I can't play the piano.

FRITZ: I know it, I just can't remember it.

MIZI: I'll sing it for you.

THEODORE: Brings back fond memories no doubt.

(MIZI, *beginning to sing, leads* FRITZ *into the tune.** MIZI *sings the chorus and then starts the verse with the others,* *particularly* THEODORE, *contributing the bits they know. When the song reaches the chorus for the second time,* THEODORE *gets up and dances with* MIZI. *Meanwhile* CHRISTINE *joins* FRITZ *at the piano.*)

The False Hussar

Sweetheart, please don't send me away.
Sweetheart, there's no war on today.
Sweetheart, won't you dally, do.
Or I'll die
Or I'll die for love of you.

Hail and farewell, my gay Hussar.
Handsome and bold and brave you are.
How many girls did you forsake?
Here is one heart that you won't break!
Even with all your gallantry
Here you will have no victory.
What is it that you're waiting for?
Shouldn't you be at war?

Sweetheart, please don't send me away.
Sweetheart, there's no war on today.
Sweetheart, won't you dally, do.
Or I'll die
Or I'll die for love of you.

(*At the end of the second chorus the doorbell is heard.* FRITZ *stops playing. The dancers, however, carry on heedlessly. Then they realize that the music has stopped.*)
Has somebody shot the piano player?
FRITZ: That was the door. Did you invite anyone else?
THEODORE: Of course not. You don't have to answer it.

*The tune used in the original National Theatre production was 'Don't Be So Naughty' from *Der Obersteiger* by Karl Millöcker. The words, however, were invented for the occasion; as was the title.

CHRISTINE: What's the matter?

FRITZ: Nothing.

(THEODORE *and* MIZI *pick up the dance to their own accompaniment. The doorbell rings again.*)

THEODORE: You're not at home.

FRITZ: You can hear the piano out in the hall. And anyone can see the lights from the street.

THEODORE: What nonsense. You're simply not at home.

FRITZ: But it puts me off.

THEODORE: So what do you think it is – a letter? A telegram?

FRITZ: Damn it, I'll have to go and see.

(FRITZ *goes out to the door.*)

MIZI: How boring!

(*She thumps the piano keys discordantly.*)

THEODORE: Oh, do stop! (*To* CHRISTINE) What's the matter? Has the doorbell put you off too?

(FRITZ *re-enters, closing the door behind him.*)

CHRISTINE: Who was it?

FRITZ: Would you be good enough to give me a few moments . . . Would you mind going into the next room?

THEODORE: Oh no!

CHRISTINE: Who is it?

FRITZ: Nothing, my love – I just have to have a few words with someone.

(*The two women allow themselves to be shown into the kitchen by* THEODORE.)

THEODORE: (*To* FRITZ) Get rid of her.

FRITZ: Go on – get in!

(FRITZ *goes out to the front door. After a few moments the* GENTLEMAN *enters. He is wearing officer's uniform.*)

I must apologize for keeping you waiting. Please . . .

GENTLEMAN: Not at all. I'm sorry to have disturbed you.

FRITZ: You haven't at all.

GENTLEMAN: Oh, but I can see I have. A little gathering?

FRITZ: Just a few of the chaps.

GENTLEMAN: (*Still friendly*) Sounds a bit dubious.

FRITZ: (*Awkwardly*) I beg your pardon?

GENTLEMAN: They seem to go in for feather boas and picture hats.

FRITZ: Oh yes. (*Smiles.*) One or two of them *are* a bit dubious.

GENTLEMAN: Life can be so amusing sometimes.

FRITZ: May I make so bold as to inquire to what I owe the honour of this . . . Why have you come?

GENTLEMAN: (*Calmly*) My wife left one of her gloves here . . .

FRITZ: Your wife? Here? There must be some mistake.

GENTLEMAN: My wife left one of her gloves here – a glove like this one.

(*The* GENTLEMAN *slaps* FRITZ *on the face with the glove.*

FRITZ *takes a step back. Pause.*)

Well? I said – well? A Yellow Dragoon.

(FRITZ *snaps to attention.*)

FRITZ: I am at your disposal.

GENTLEMAN: And I shall dispose of you.

(*The* GENTLEMAN *produces a bundle of letters.*)

Here are your letters. I must ask you to give me those you have received. I wouldn't want them to be found here . . . afterwards.

FRITZ: They won't be found.

(FRITZ *stares at him. Pause.*)

Is there anything more I can do for you?

GENTLEMAN: Anything more? That *you* might do for *me*?

(*The* GENTLEMAN *turns to leave, then changes his mind.*)

You young know-it-alls . . . take-it-alls . . . My box, my table, my – You grab – brag – strut – rut like dogs in the street – and you'll be shot down like dogs.

FRITZ: I am at your disposal.

GENTLEMAN: (*Bows coldly.*) Good.

FRITZ: I am entirely at your disposal. I shall be at home tomorrow until noon.

GENTLEMAN: Ah – about tomorrow. My wife's musical evening.

FRITZ: Please ask her to forgive me.

23

GENTLEMAN: I'm sure she will miss you.

FRITZ: Perhaps another time.

GENTLEMAN: Yes, perhaps. After all I might miss you too.

> (*The* GENTLEMAN *turns to leave.* FRITZ *moves to see him out but the* GENTLEMAN *stops him with a gesture. The* GENTLEMAN *lets himself out.* FRITZ *stands for a moment and then goes to the window and peers through it. He goes to the kitchen door and opens it a little.*)

FRITZ: Theo, a moment.

> (THEODORE *enters, closing the door behind him.*)

THEODORE: All right?

FRITZ: It was him.

THEODORE: Ah! I hope you didn't do anything silly.

FRITZ: He knows.

THEODORE: He knows nothing. He laid a trap for you, and you fell for it. You're a fool . . .

> (FRITZ *shows* THEODORE *the letters.*)

Ah. I've always said one shouldn't put it in writing.

FRITZ: That must have been him outside this afternoon.

THEODORE: Well, tell me what happened.

FRITZ: Theodore, I have the honour to ask of you a certain favour –

THEODORE: Oh, do stop talking like that. I'll straighten it out.

FRITZ: It's got beyond that.

THEODORE: We'll see.

FRITZ: Anyway it would be as well if you . . . but we can't keep those poor girls waiting any longer –

THEODORE: Let them wait. What were you going to say?

FRITZ: It would be as well if you went and got Lensky before the night's out.

THEODORE: I'll go now if you like.

FRITZ: You won't get him now. But he'll be in the café between eleven and twelve – you could both come round then.

THEODORE: Don't look like that. Nine times out of ten it all comes out all right.

FRITZ: This time it won't. He'll make sure of that.

THEODORE: Oh, but think of that business last year between Dr Billinger and Herz – same thing exactly.

FRITZ: Come on, you know as well as I do he might as well have shot me dead here in this room. It would have come to the same thing.

THEODORE: Oh, yes – what a wonderful attitude. And Lensky and I count for nothing? Do you think we'll let –

FRITZ: I don't want any of that. Let him have what he wants.

THEODORE: Fritz –

FRITZ: What's the point, Theodore? As if you didn't know yourself.

THEODORE: Nonsense. Anyway there's a lot of luck in these things – you're just as likely to – almost as likely – there's a fair chance – oh God!

FRITZ: She felt it coming. We both did. We knew it.

THEODORE: Enough of that.

FRITZ: What in God's name is she doing at this moment? I wonder if he . . . Theodore, tomorrow you've got to find out what's going on there.

THEODORE: I'll do my best.

FRITZ: And make sure there's no delay.

THEODORE: It can't be before the day after tomorrow.

FRITZ: Theodore!

THEODORE: Don't despair – I'm positive that everything will turn out all right – don't ask me why but intuition counts for something. It just struck me, I felt it in my bones – I mean my heart – (*Apologetically he 'shoots' himself in the head for his* faux pas *and then realizes how much worse he has made matters*) – oh God, sorry!

(FRITZ *and* THEODORE *catch the humour of the moment and laugh together.*)

FRITZ: You're a real friend. But what on earth are we going to tell the girls?

THEODORE: Does it matter? Let's get rid of them.

FRITZ: Oh no. We must be cheerful as can be. I'll go back to the piano and you call them in. What will you tell them?

THEODORE: To mind their own business.

FRITZ: No . . .

THEODORE: I'll tell them it concerns a pal of yours, we'll think of something.

(THEODORE *opens the door.*)

Ladies . . .

FRITZ: Theo – what a relief, eh?

(MIZI *and* CHRISTINE *enter.*)

MIZI: At last!

CHRISTINE: Who was it, Fritz?

THEODORE: Curiosity killed the cat –

(FRITZ *begins to play the funeral march.*)

CHRISTINE: Tell me, Fritz – please.

FRITZ: Sweetheart, I can't. It concerns people you don't know at all.

CHRISTINE: What people?

THEODORE: She won't leave you in peace. Don't tell her a thing – you gave him your word.

CHRISTINE: Him? Oh, you mean . . .

MIZI: Leave off, Christine – don't be a bore. Let them have their little pleasures, they're only trying to make it sound important.

THEODORE: Mizi and I have to finish our dance – maestro, music if you please!

(THEODORE *and* MIZI *dance for a few moments but the mood has gone wrong.*)

MIZI: I can't any more.

(THEODORE *kisses her and sits on the arm of the chair.* FRITZ *stays at the piano. He takes* CHRISTINE's *hands and looks at her.*)

CHRISTINE: Why have you stopped?

FRITZ: Enough for tonight.

CHRISTINE: That's how I'd like to be able to play.

FRITZ: Do you play much?

CHRISTINE: I don't get much chance. There's always so much to do at home. And then we've got such a terrible piano.

FRITZ: I'd like to play it some time, and to see your room.

CHRISTINE: It's not as nice as here.

FRITZ: And there's something else I want. I want you to tell me everything about yourself. I know so little.

CHRISTINE: Little is all there is. And I don't have any secrets either – unlike some people I know.

FRITZ: Never been in love?

(CHRISTINE *looks at him.* FRITZ *kisses her hand.*)

CHRISTINE: And I'll never love anyone else.

FRITZ: You mustn't say that . . . ever . . . how can you know? Do you always tell your father everything, Christine?

CHRISTINE: Not any more.

FRITZ: Don't feel bad about it, little one. In the end we all have our secrets. That's how we live.

CHRISTINE: If only I knew that you really cared for me, everything would be all right.

FRITZ: Don't you know?

CHRISTINE: When you talk to me like this I think I do.

FRITZ: Christine . . . you can't be comfortable like that.

CHRISTINE: Oh, no, please, let me stay. I'm all right.

(FRITZ *strokes her hair.*)

Oh. Oh – that's nice.

(*Silence.*)

THEODORE: So, Fritz, where's the cigar cupboard?

(THEODORE *exits, then comes back immediately with coffee on a tray.*)

Who's for black coffee?

FRITZ: Mizi –

THEODORE: Let her sleep. And you shouldn't be drinking black coffee. You ought to get to bed as soon as possible and make sure of a good night's rest.

(FRITZ *glances at him and laughs bitterly.*)

Well, that's the way things are. Whether you've behaved well or badly is no longer the point. Behaving sensibly is all that counts.

FRITZ: You will bring Lensky tonight, won't you?

THEODORE: There's no need. Tomorrow is soon enough.

FRITZ: I'm asking you.

THEODORE: Then I will.

FRITZ: Will you see the girls home?

THEODORE: Yes – and right now. Mizi – up you get!

> (MIZI *has fallen asleep. She stirs now.*)

MIZI: Is that black coffee? Can I have some?

THEODORE: Here we are, my dear.

FRITZ: (*To* CHRISTINE) Tired, little girl?

CHRISTINE: Oh, I love it when you talk to me like that.

FRITZ: So tired . . .

CHRISTINE: It's the wine. And it's given me a bit of a headache.

FRITZ: Some fresh air will put that right.

CHRISTINE: Are we going already? Are you coming with us?

FRITZ: No, darling – I shall stay at home now. I've a few things to do.

CHRISTINE: Now? What could you have to do at this time?

FRITZ: (*Almost sternly*) Christine, you must stop doing that . . . (*More kindly*) Actually I'm dead beat – Theo and I were tramping round the countryside for hours today.

THEODORE: Oh, it was glorious. We'll all go out in the country together one day soon.

MIZI: Oh, that'll be devastating – and you've both got to put on your uniforms.

THEODORE: She has a real feeling for nature.

CHRISTINE: (*To* FRITZ) When will I see you?

FRITZ: I'll write.

CHRISTINE: (*Sadly*) Well, goodbye then.

> (*She turns to go.* FRITZ *notices her sadness.*)

FRITZ: Christine. We'll see each other tomorrow then.

CHRISTINE: (*Eagerly*) Really?

FRITZ: The railway gardens. Same as before. Let's say six o'clock. Will that be all right?

MIZI: Aren't you coming with us, we want to be dragooned!

THEODORE: The woman's obsessed.

FRITZ: No, I'm staying here.

MIZI: Lucky you – we've got quite a trek.

FRITZ: Wait, Mizi – you're leaving nearly all the cakes behind – you must take them home with you.

MIZI: Is that allowed?

CHRISTINE: Honestly, she's like a child.

MIZI: Wait a minute – for that I'll help you blow out the candles.

CHRISTINE: Should I open a window? It's so stuffy in here.

FRITZ: Yes, we can go out that way. There you are, children.

MIZI: Are the street lights out already?

THEODORE: Of course they are.

FRITZ: I'll light the way out for you.

CHRISTINE: Oh how wonderful to have some air.

MIZI: Go on, out you go, quick march – get along with you.

(*There is a general exit through the french doors.* FRITZ *holds aloft one of the candelabra to light the way. He stands watching as they disappear chattering and laughing together. They pick up the tune of 'The False Hussar' as they go. Standing outside on the terrace,* FRITZ *picks up one of his discarded targets. He walks back into the room, holding up the target, looking for the bullet hole. He moves the target behind the candles for a better look. The target catches fire. He stands holding the candelabra in one hand, and the blazing target in the other, the only light now in the room.*)

ACT TWO

*The living room of the top-floor flat shared by Christine and her father.
It is simply furnished. There are a few books in a bookcase. There is a
window with a view over the rooftops. There is also a roof terrace. There
is a large stove on which there is a bust of Schubert.*

*A silver band can be heard playing distantly in the park. Occasionally
from nearer at hand a clanking goods train is heard to pass by below.
The room is empty. Then* CHRISTINE *hurries in from within, in the
process of getting dressed, carrying a hat and an artificial flower. She
hurries to a sewing box and starts sewing the flower on to the hat.
A knock at the door leading to the stairs is followed by* FRAU
BINDER *calling* 'Herr Weiring!' FRAU BINDER *enters (and
perhaps helps* CHRISTINE *to finish dressing during the first part of
the dialogue).*

FRAU BINDER: Yoo hoo, Herr Weiring!

CHRISTINE: Oh – Frau Binder!

FRAU BINDER: Good evening, Christine.
    (*She appraises* CHRISTINE.)
    Oh, you look . . .
    (*She sniffs* CHRISTINE's *perfume.*)
    Going out?

CHRISTINE: How are you? – Is everything well downstairs?

FRAU BINDER: Yes, you're quite a stranger. In fact, my
husband was wondering if you'd join us for dinner in the
Lehnergarten as it's the night the band plays.

CHRISTINE: Thank you very much, Frau Binder, but I can't
this evening. Another time, perhaps. You don't mind, do
you?

FRAU BINDER: Why should I mind? You'll have a much nicer
time without us. Your father's left for the theatre?

CHRISTINE: Oh no, he'll be home soon. It's a piano rehearsal
and the orchestra isn't called tonight.

FRAU BINDER: In that case I'll wait for him. I've been meaning to ask him for ages for some tickets. I suppose one can get some now?

CHRISTINE: Oh yes, but why not come to the dress rehearsal in a couple of days? I'll be there too.

FRAU BINDER: If people like us didn't have friends in the theatre we'd never get to go. But don't let me keep you, Christine. My husband will be disappointed of course – not to mention someone else.

CHRISTINE: Who's that?

FRAU BINDER: Binder's cousin is joining us. Did you know Franz has a steady job now, Christine?

CHRISTINE: Oh, really?

FRAU BINDER: Good money, too. Such a nice young man. And he thinks the world of you, you know.

CHRISTINE: Well, I have to be off, Frau Binder.

FRAU BINDER: He won't listen to a word against you – whatever they say. There *are* men who –

CHRISTINE: Goodbye, Frau Binder.

FRAU BINDER: Goodbye. Don't keep the young man waiting!

CHRISTINE: Is something the matter, Frau Binder?

FRAU BINDER: Nothing at all – you're quite right, you're only young once.

CHRISTINE: Goodbye, then.

FRAU BINDER: Only, you ought to be a bit more discreet.

CHRISTINE: What do you mean?

FRAU BINDER: Vienna is big enough to hide a multitude of – I mean, why do you have to meet him a hundred yards from your own door?

CHRISTINE: I don't think that's anyone else's business.

FRAU BINDER: I couldn't believe my ears when Binder told me. He saw you. Get on with you, I said to him, you're imagining things. Christine isn't the sort of girl who romps around in the dark with young men. And if she did get up to something she'd certainly know enough not to do it on her own doorstep. Well, he said, you can ask her yourself.

And, he said, who's to wonder – she doesn't come in to see
us any more, instead she goes about with that Mizi Schlager
. . . hardly fit company for a nice girl. Men have such dirty
minds, Christine. And of course he felt it was his duty to
tell Franz straight away and Franz turned on him. He'd go
through fire for his Christine and anyone who says a word
against her gets an earful, about how good you are in the
house, how kind you always were to auntie, God rest her
soul, how well brought up you are and so on . . . Won't
you change your mind and come with us to listen to the
music?

CHRISTINE: No.

(CHRISTINE's *father*, HERR WEIRING, *enters holding a sprig
of lilac*.)

HERR WEIRING: Good evening – oh, Frau Binder, how are
you?

FRAU BINDER: Quite well, thank you.

HERR WEIRING: And how's little Lina? And your husband?

FRAU BINDER: Both well, thanks be to God.

HERR WEIRING: That's good. (*To* CHRISTINE) Still indoors on
such a lovely evening?

CHRISTINE: I was just on my way.

HERR WEIRING: That's right, it's lovely out in the fresh air.
Don't you think so, Frau Binder? Really marvellous. I've
just come by the railway gardens. The lilac is out. A
magnificent sight. I've been guilty of a misdemeanour.
(*He gives the flower to* CHRISTINE.)

CHRISTINE: Thank you, father.

FRAU BINDER: You're lucky the park-keeper didn't see you.

HERR WEIRING: You should go too, Frau Binder. The scent of
the lilac is so strong you won't miss this little sprig.

FRAU BINDER: If everyone thought like that –

HERR WEIRING: Yes, that would be too bad –

CHRISTINE: I'll see you later, father.

HERR WEIRING: Should I come with you?

CHRISTINE: Well, I . . . I promised to see Mizi.

HERR WEIRING: Ah yes, a much better idea. Youth must be served. Goodbye, then.

CHRISTINE: Goodbye, Frau Binder.

(CHRISTINE *goes. Her father looks after her tenderly.*)

FRAU BINDER: She's very thick with that Mizi.

HERR WEIRING: I'm glad she has someone to go about with instead of sitting around the house – it's not much of a life for the poor girl.

FRAU BINDER: Yes, I suppose so.

HERR WEIRING: I can't tell you, Frau Binder, how sad it makes me when I come home from a rehearsal and find her sitting here like Cinderella . . . and after lunch we are hardly up from the table before she's sat down again with her music scores.

FRAU BINDER: Oh, yes, we'd all rather be millionaires. But what about her singing?

HERR WEIRING: It won't get her very far. Her voice is good enough for the family piano – music to a father's ears – but she'll never make a living with it.

FRAU BINDER: Such a shame.

HERR WEIRING: I'm glad she knows it – at least she won't be disappointed.

FRAU BINDER: Oh, girls are such a worry! I came up to invite her to come and hear the band in the Lehnergarten. I thought it might cheer her up a bit. She could do with it.

HERR WEIRING: Why didn't she want to go?

FRAU BINDER: I don't know. I think perhaps because Binder's cousin is coming with us.

HERR WEIRING: Oh that'll be it – she can't bear him. She told me.

FRAU BINDER: Why not? Franz is a perfectly decent young man. He's got a steady job now. These days that's not to be sneezed at by a . . .

HERR WEIRING: By a poor girl, you were going to say?

FRAU BINDER: By any girl.

HERR WEIRING: Come now, Frau Binder – a girl in the

springtime of her life, is that what girls like her are meant for
– decent young men with steady jobs?

FRAU BINDER: (*Surprised*) Yes. One can't wait for Prince
Charming to turn up and if some day he comes along he'll
ask for everything but her hand and be off again. That's why
I always say one can't be too careful with a young girl,
especially in the company she keeps.

HERR WEIRING: So she's supposed to throw her youth out of the
window, is she? And what does the poor thing get out of all
this decency if she ends up as the wife of a haberdasher?

FRAU BINDER: Herr Weiring, my husband may be a haberdasher
but he's a decent and respectable man who has never given
me cause for complaint.

HERR WEIRING: Oh, but Frau Binder – did I mean you? You
didn't throw your youth out of the window.

FRAU BINDER: I really can't remember.

HERR WEIRING: Oh, don't say that – say what you like but
memories are the most precious things we have.

FRAU BINDER: I have none.

HERR WEIRING: Oh, come now.

FRAU BINDER: And what has one got to show for it if they're the
sort of memories you're talking about? Nothing but regrets.

HERR WEIRING: And what has one got to show for it if one
doesn't even have those? If one's whole life has just drifted
by, one day after another, one day like another, without joy,
without love . . . you think that's any better?

FRAU BINDER: Well, think of your sister.

HERR WEIRING: Yes. Think of her.

FRAU BINDER: Well, aren't you glad that the poor thing always
had you to protect her? You were a brother in a thousand –
(*He protests.*)
– no, it's true, you had to be mother and father to her when
you were hardly more than a boy.

HERR WEIRING: Yes, at least I had that excuse. I thought I knew
what was best for her. Like God. But as time went on and
her hair turned grey and her face got lined, and the days

34

followed one another and her youth passed with them till
my pretty sister was suddenly an old maid – only then did I
realize what I had done.

FRAU BINDER: Oh, but Herr Weiring – !

HERR WEIRING: I can still see her, the way she sat opposite me
in the evenings by that lamp there – smiling at me with a
gentle resignation, as if she wanted to thank me for
something. And I ought to have gone down on my knees
and asked her forgiveness for protecting her so thoroughly
from any chance of happiness.

FRAU BINDER: Or unhappiness. How is one supposed to know?
My husband – (*She changes her mind.*) My husband will be
waiting for me. I say, why don't *you* come with us?

HERR WEIRING: Perhaps I might.

FRAU BINDER: But do take your overcoat, it'll get quite chilly
later on.

HERR WEIRING: Do you think so?

FRAU BINDER: Of course it will – How can you take so little
care of yourself?
(HERR WEIRING *takes his coat and they leave together.*)
(*As they leave*) And how is the new show?

HERR WEIRING: Charming. So pretty. So true to life.
(*This takes them out. The distant music reasserts itself and the
evening fades a little.*)

CHRISTINE *returns, disappointed. She has closed the door behind
her. There is a knock at the door. She ignores it, and starts to leave
the room in the direction of the interior. She is halted by the sound of*
MIZI's *voice calling her name and the door opening.*

MIZI: I was chasing you up the road. Didn't you hear me?

CHRISTINE: No.

MIZI: What's the matter?

CHRISTINE: Nothing. Bit of a headache.

MIZI: It's all that wine last night – I'm amazed I haven't got
one. Still, it was fun wasn't it? They're a terrific couple of
swells, aren't they? And that's a devastating place Fritz has

got, *très élégant*. Now, Dory's place – whoops! – enough of that!

CHRISTINE: Oh, Mizi, what do you think – he never turned up.

MIZI: He stood you up? Well, serves you right!

CHRISTINE: What do you mean? What have I done?

MIZI: You throw yourself at him and let him walk all over you. It makes them too sure of themselves.

CHRISTINE: What do you know about it?

MIZI: It's the only thing I do know about. You make me cross sometimes. He doesn't show up, he doesn't walk you home, shares a box with strangers and goes off with them, and you gaze at him like a lovesick duck.

CHRISTINE: Don't talk like that – stop acting rottener than you are. You know you like Theodore too.

MIZI: Like him – of course I like him. But I'm not going to put myself out for him – not for Dory or anyone else. Not all the men in the world are worth it put together and certainly not one at a time.

CHRISTINE: Mizi, I don't know you like this.

MIZI: I took care you wouldn't. I was a bit in awe of you. But all the same I did think – when it hits her it will knock her sideways. The first time always does. But you can be glad of one thing, you had a friend like me around.

CHRISTINE: Mizi!

MIZI: Do you think I'm not? What would you take it into your head to do if you didn't have me to tell you? Men are all the same and the lot of them aren't worth one unhappy hour. Let me tell you, girl – you can't believe a thing men say.

CHRISTINE: Why do you keep talking about *men*? – I'm not interested in any of the others! For the rest of my life I'll only care about one man!

MIZI: You won't. The record stands at eighteen months. All the rest is front.

CHRISTINE: Oh, please stop!

MIZI: Maybe there is a man who would devote himself to you for life but only a fool would look for him in Vienna.

36

CHRISTINE: Mizi – don't –

MIZI: And only a cretin would look for him in the Medical School, and only you in the Dragoons.

CHRISTINE: Mizi – I can't bear to listen to this today – it hurts me –

MIZI: Oh, come on –

CHRISTINE: I'd rather you went. I'm sorry. I'd rather be left alone.

(CHRISTINE *goes out on to the roof terrace.*)

MIZI: I'm off. Come and see me at the theatre when you're better. Perhaps that's my trouble – no man is a hero to a wardrobe mistress. They're all the same when they're waiting for their trousers.

(*She turns to go and finds that* FRITZ *has appeared in the doorway. He looks at her inquiringly. She jerks her head towards the door leading to the roof.* FRITZ *comes further into the room.* MIZI *offers him her hand.* FRITZ *raises her hand to his lips and bows over it.* MIZI *kisses him passionately on the mouth. He is taken by surprise, disconcerted, and he pushes her away. She laughs at him and leaves, still laughing.* FRITZ *looks carefully around the room and then approaches the piano. He lifts the lid and plays a tune with one finger.* CHRISTINE *hears this and comes to the door and sees him.*)

FRITZ: Hello!

CHRISTINE: (*Joyously*) Fritz! Oh, Fritz!

(*She rushes into his arms.*)

FRITZ: Steady on – darling!

CHRISTINE: Everybody says you'll drop me but you won't, will you? Not yet – not yet –

FRITZ: Who says so? What's all this?

(*He calms her, stroking her.*)

Well, honestly, my darling – I thought you'd be a bit put out to see me up here.

CHRISTINE: As long as you're here – nothing else matters.

FRITZ: There, there – calm down.

CHRISTINE: Why didn't you come?

FRITZ: I did. I came late. I waited in the gardens but I couldn't see you and I was about to give up and go home when I suddenly felt such a desperation – such a longing to see this dear little face . . .

CHRISTINE: Is that true?

FRITZ: And then I suddenly had to see where you lived – yes, I really did – I just had to see it once, I couldn't wait, so I came straight up – you don't mind?

CHRISTINE: Oh God!

FRITZ: No one saw me.

CHRISTINE: What do I care!

FRITZ: (*Looking round*) So here it is. So this is your room. It's so . . . nice.

CHRISTINE: But you can't see anything.
(*She is about to take the shade off the lamp to light it.*)

FRITZ: No, let it be. I don't want the light in my eyes. It's better as it is. So this is where you are. This is the table you told me about where you sit and work. And what a view – over so many rooftops – and over there – what's that dark mass. . . ?

CHRISTINE: That's the Kahlenberg.

FRITZ: Of course! You're much better off than I am!

CHRISTINE: Oh. . . !

FRITZ: I'd love to live as high as this and look out over the rooftops. It's marvellous. And how quiet this street must be.

CHRISTINE: Oh, it's quite noisy enough during the day.

FRITZ: Do you get much traffic going by?

CHRISTINE: No, but there's the railway –

FRITZ: Oh, I shouldn't like that.

CHRISTINE: You get used to it and after a while you stop hearing it.

FRITZ: Is it really the first time I've been here? Everything seems so familiar – it's exactly as I'd imagined it –

CHRISTINE: Oh, don't look too closely –

FRITZ: What are those pictures?

CHRISTINE: No – don't!

FRITZ: But I'd like to see them.

CHRISTINE: *Hail* and *Farewell*.

FRITZ: So they are. *Hail* and *Farewell*.

CHRISTINE: I know very well they aren't great art –

FRITZ: (*Another painting*) And what's this? *Forsaken*! Poor girl!

CHRISTINE: It's those Dragoons, I expect.

FRITZ: And who's the old boy up there on the stove?

CHRISTINE: That's Schubert of course.

FRITZ: So it is.

CHRISTINE: Because father's so fond of him. My father used to compose songs himself once, beautiful songs which he would teach me . . .

FRITZ: Not any more?

CHRISTINE: Not any more.

FRITZ: Ah – and here's your collection of books.

CHRISTINE: Don't look at those.

FRITZ: Why not? Schiller! . . . and Goethe . . . and an encyclopaedia. Well, well!

CHRISTINE: It only goes up to G.

FRITZ: So it does. *Everybody's Encyclopaedia*. You look at the pictures, do you?

CHRISTINE: What do you mean, Fritz?

FRITZ: You look at the pictures. In the encyclopaedia. You like to look at the pictures.

CHRISTINE: Well, yes, I look at the pictures too.

FRITZ: Oh – I didn't mean – it's only because I love your pretty little head, and I don't want it bothered about . . . I've said the wrong thing.

CHRISTINE: Oh, no Fritz – ! I love you loving my head – if you like I'll never read anything again!

FRITZ: It's so cosy here.

CHRISTINE: Do you really like it?

FRITZ: Very much. And what's this?

CHRISTINE: Now what's he found!

FRITZ: Oh no, dear girl, these don't belong here – they're faded . . .

(FRITZ *has picked up a vase containing artificial flowers.*)

CHRISTINE: I'm sure they're not.

FRITZ: Artificial flowers always look faded. You should have real flowers in your room – fresh and fragrant. I'll make sure that from now on . . .
(*He breaks off.*)

CHRISTINE: What? What were you going to say?

FRITZ: Nothing.

CHRISTINE: Tell me.

FRITZ: I was only going to say that I'll send you some flowers tomorrow.

CHRISTINE: Well, and do you take it back already? Of course! – by tomorrow you'll have forgotten all about me.

FRITZ: What are you talking about?

CHRISTINE: Oh yes – I know – I can feel it.

FRITZ: How can you think that of me?

CHRISTINE: It's because of you. You make such a secret of yourself. You don't tell me anything about yourself. How do you spend your days?

FRITZ: But darling, it's all very ordinary. I go to lectures – well, sometimes – and I go to the coffee house – I read – I play the piano – I pass the time with people . . . it's all quite trivial, too boring to talk about.

CHRISTINE: But you must have done lots of other things.

FRITZ: No. Not really. That's all I've ever done. And now my time is up. I have to go, my flower.

CHRISTINE: Already?

FRITZ: Your father will be home.

CHRISTINE: Not for hours yet, Fritz – stay a bit longer – only for a minute – do stay!

FRITZ: The other thing is, I have to . . . Theodore's expecting me. There's something I have to discuss with him.

CHRISTINE: Does it have to be today?

FRITZ: I'm afraid it does.

CHRISTINE: You can see him tomorrow.

FRITZ: I may not be in Vienna tomorrow.

CHRISTINE: Not in Vienna!?

FRITZ: Well, yes. It's been known to happen. I might go away
for the day – even two days – you funny little girl –

CHRISTINE: Where to?

FRITZ: Where to? Here or there. Heavens, don't look like that.
I'm going down to my parents. Is there anything wrong
with that?

CHRISTINE: You see! You're secretive about them, too.

FRITZ: What a baby you are! I can't tell you how lovely it is
being alone here with you. Don't you think it's nice?

CHRISTINE: No, I don't. It isn't nice being told nothing – don't
you see? I want to know everything about you. Every little
thing. It isn't enough to have you for an hour on the
occasional evening – and then you're off again and I'm no
wiser. And the whole night to get through and another day,
hour after hour, still knowing nothing. It makes me
unhappy.

FRITZ: But why should it?

CHRISTINE: Well, it's because I miss you so much and you might
as well not be living in the same city – you could be somewhere
else entirely! You seem so far away it's as if you're dead!

FRITZ: Christine –

CHRISTINE: No, it's true!

FRITZ: Come here a moment.

(CHRISTINE *comes close to him.*)

There's only one thing you can really know – that you love
me *now*. At this moment. Don't look beyond. Sometimes a
moment seems to contain the whole of beyond inside it –
but that's as close as we come to knowing eternity. It's the
only glimpse we get.

(*He kisses her. He gets up. Suddenly he bursts out.*)

Oh, how lovely it is being here with you! How lovely. One
feels so secret here, tucked away among all these rooftops
and chimneys, so protected, so alone. So safe.

CHRISTINE: If you always spoke to me like that I could almost
believe . . .

FRITZ: What, dear?

CHRISTINE: That you love me as much as I dreamed you did the first time you kissed me. Do you remember?

FRITZ: I do love you.

(*He kisses her and then breaks away.*)

But now let me go –

CHRISTINE: Are you already sorry you said it? After all, you're free. You're free. You can drop me if you want. You made no promises and I made no conditions. What happens to me doesn't matter – I've been happy once and it's all I ask of life. I only want you to know that I never loved anyone before you and when you don't want me any more I'll never love anyone else.

FRITZ: Don't say that – don't – it's too – (*distastefully*) it's like that picture –

CHRISTINE: (*Hurt*) I realize your taste is above such sentiment – these clichés –

FRITZ: Oh, Christine – everything tastes bitter to me now! I'm so sorry I hurt you – please don't, don't cry, Christine, Christine.

(*They embrace. There is a bold knock at the door.* CHRISTINE *and* FRITZ *fearfully break apart.* CHRISTINE *lights the lamp while* FRITZ *steps outside on to the roof terrace. There is another knock and* THEODORE *enters.*)

THEODORE: Hello – I've got a nerve, haven't I?

FRITZ: (*Emerging*) Have you got something to tell me?

THEODORE: I have.

CHRISTINE: It must be something very important.

THEODORE: It is.

FRITZ: So . . . you're with me tomorrow?

THEODORE: That's right.

FRITZ: Good. Why didn't you wait downstairs?

CHRISTINE: What's all this whispering?

THEODORE: Why didn't I wait downstairs? Well, if I'd been sure you were up here . . . I wasn't going to risk walking up and down for two hours. I've been looking for him everywhere. I've been run off my feet so I must beg a glass of water.

CHRISTINE: I'll get one.

(CHRISTINE *leaves the room.*)

THEODORE: What are you doing here?

FRITZ: Is there any more news?

THEODORE: What?

FRITZ: About her.

THEODORE: Who? Oh, no. I only came to collect you because you're so irresponsible. What's all this excitement? You ought to be resting, this is no place for you.

FRITZ: You're right. God, how such moments deceive us.

THEODORE: What moments?

FRITZ: I almost believed that my happiness is with that girl. But it's one big lie.

THEODORE: Sentimental rot.

FRITZ: Yes. That's right, rot. Sweetness and decay, they go together.

THEODORE: You'll laugh at it tomorrow.

FRITZ: I doubt I'll get the chance.

(CHRISTINE *re-enters with the water.*)

Don't you think this room is lovely?

THEODORE: Yes, very nice. Are you stuck here all day? I mean, it's very cosy but it's a bit high up for my liking.

FRITZ: That's just what I love about it.

(THEODORE *drinks some of the water and gives the glass back to* CHRISTINE.)

THEODORE: But now I have to take Fritz away. We have to be up early tomorrow.

CHRISTINE: So you really are going away.

THEODORE: He'll be back, Christine!

CHRISTINE: Will you write to me?

THEODORE: He's not going far.

CHRISTINE: Oh, but I know he is. You are, Fritz. Never mind.

THEODORE: This is nonsense, Christine. She doesn't know what she's saying. All right then, kiss each other goodbye since

43

it's going to seem like for ever – oh God! – pretend I'm not here. Take as long as you like.

(FRITZ *and* CHRISTINE *kiss.*)

Right, that's enough! Goodbye, Christine.

FRITZ: (*To* CHRISTINE) I don't want to go.

CHRISTINE: Oh, get on with you – you're just being silly.

THEODORE: She's absolutely right.

FRITZ: (*Turning on him angrily*) Theo, it's my life!

(THEODORE, *taken aback, hesitates and then leaves.* FRITZ *takes* CHRISTINE *in his arms.*)

ACT THREE

We are backstage at the Josefstadt theatre, the wings providing our
forestage with a partial view of the Josefstadt stage beyond.
The transition between Act Two and Act Three should be made
without an intermission. The effect should be that the scenery of Act
Two should now be seen to be cleared from the stage of the Josefstadt
by the opera stage-hands. The stage-hands get the space into a
'rehearsal state' while the orchestra, unseen, is tuning up.
The characters in the rehearsal are to be a Hussar (TENOR) and a
girl (SOPRANO). They are in resplendent costume. They will be
rehearsing a duet – 'The False Hussar'. The transition is being
supervised by a STAGE MANAGER. During the transition
CHRISTINE hurries on holding sheets of music. She hands these to
the STAGE MANAGER, or possibly to an orchestra manager.

STAGE MANAGER: Are those the corrections?
CHRISTINE: Yes, can I watch the rehearsal from here?
STAGE MANAGER: Yes, all right.
    (*He takes the pages off stage, towards the orchestra. 'The False*
    Hussar' gets under way. It begins with a verse which we did not
    hear in Act One, as follows:)
TENOR: (*Sings:*) Beautiful lady, hail to thee
       Surely an angel you must be
       How can a man believe his eyes?
       How came you here from paradise?
       Angel be mine and I'll be yours
       Home have I come from foreign wars
       Fighting the Turks on land and sea
       Will you not comfort me?
    (*The TENOR is without his tunic. This is brought on by MIZI,*
    who hurries in during this first verse.)
CHRISTINE: Mizi, have you heard anything?
MIZI: What? – Oh, them. How should I know? Too busy.

(MIZI *takes the tunic 'on stage' and as the* SOPRANO *starts singing the chorus she fits the Hussar's tunic on to the* TENOR, *helping him to do it up.*)

SOPRANO: (*Sings:*) Mother told me all about you
    Mother told me what I should do
    Mother said it's all Liebelei
    Daughter mine
    Daughter mine, you must reply –

CHRISTINE: No message? Nothing?

MIZI: No.

CHRISTINE: And you've had no letter?

MIZI: Why should I get a letter?

CHRISTINE: It's been two days.

MIZI: Exactly. Two days, what's the fuss? You look awful. You're father's bound to notice you've been crying.

CHRISTINE: I've told him.

MIZI: What?

CHRISTINE: Everything.

MIZI: Well, what's the difference? One only has to look at you anyway. Does he know who it is?

CHRISTINE: Yes. I told him last night.

MIZI: What did he say?

CHRISTINE: Nothing. He wasn't angry.

MIZI: He must think Fritz will marry you.

(*The* SOPRANO *has now sung the chorus and her own verse, which is the same verse* MIZI *sang in Act One. Beginning* 'Hail and farewell, my gay Hussar'. *At the end of her verse, the* TENOR *prepares to take up his own chorus.*)

TENOR: (*Sings:*) Sweetheart, please don't send me away
    Sweetheart, there's no war on today
    Sweetheart, won't you dally, do . . .

(*But at this point there is a mishap in the rehearsal – for example, the* TENOR *knocks over some insecurely fastened part of the stage set. The song breaks down in disorder.*
STAGE-HANDS *appear to effect repairs. The* STAGE MANAGER *hurries on to apologize to the unseen 'Maestro'.*

46

MIZI *and* CHRISTINE *continue their conversation with hardly
a pause.*)

MIZI: You know what I think?

CHRISTINE: What?

MIZI: That this story of theirs about a trip is a fraud.

CHRISTINE: How?

MIZI: They probably haven't gone anywhere.

CHRISTINE: Yes, they have. I know they have. I went past his
house yesterday – the shutters were closed – he's not there.

MIZI: All right, so they're away. But they're not coming back,
not to us anyway.

CHRISTINE: You say it so calmly.

MIZI: Well, tonight or tomorrow or in six months – it all comes
to the same thing.

CHRISTINE: You don't know what you're talking about. You
don't know Fritz. He's not what you think. I saw what he
was like when he came to see me. He only pretends –
sometimes – not to care, but he loves me. Yes, I know, it's
not for ever, I do know that – but it won't stop overnight.
He's my Fritz and he'll come back.

MIZI: You've convinced me. He's probably gone to the country
to ask his aged parents for permission to marry.
(*The repair has now been made, and the duet reassembles itself
and picks up with the orchestra. The duet continues with the
beginning of the* TENOR *chorus* – 'Sweetheart, please don't
send me away'.)

CHRISTINE: Mizi . . . do me a favour.

MIZI: Don't worry so much. What do you want?

CHRISTINE: Go round to Theodore's after rehearsal. It's not
very far – just look in and ask if he's back yet. If he's not
there they might know when he's expected.

MIZI: I'm not running after any man.

CHRISTINE: He doesn't need to know anything about it.
Perhaps you'll bump into him by accident.

MIZI: Why don't you do it yourself? – go round to Fritz's place.

CHRISTINE: I daren't. He hates anything like that. And I'm

sure he can't be back. But Theodore might be and he'd know. Please, Mizi.

MIZI: You're such a baby sometimes.

CHRISTINE: Do it for me. Go on. It's not asking a lot.

MIZI: Well, if it means so much to you. But it won't do any good. They're not at home.

CHRISTINE: And you'll come and tell me?

MIZI: All right.

CHRISTINE: Thank you, Mizi, you're a friend.

MIZI: Yes, I am. Now go home and I'll see you later.

CHRISTINE: Thank you.

(*Now the duet goes wrong again, for different reasons. The* TENOR, *singing the chorus solo, explains the reason, improvising out of his song.*)

TENOR: (*Sings:*) Sweetheart, please don't send me away
Sweetheart, there's no war on today
I can't sing in this bloody thing!
It's too tight – it's far far far too tight!

(*So singing, he has taken off the tunic and tossed it back to* MIZI *who catches it and hurries away in guilty confusion to, no doubt, make it less tight. The orchestra of course has broken down. The* TENOR *leaves the stage in a huff. The* SOPRANO *follows him.* MEMBERS OF THE ORCHESTRA *start crossing our stage from the direction of the musicians' pit. Among them is* HERR WEIRING.)

HERR WEIRING: Christine –

CHRISTINE: What's the matter? What is it?

HERR WEIRING: I want you to go home. Don't stop on the way.

CHRISTINE: Father. . . ?

HERR WEIRING: Just go home.

CHRISTINE: You're angry.

HERR WEIRING: Of course not. It's my fault. Please go home. I'll come after rehearsals.

CHRISTINE: What are you talking about? What's happened? I thought you understood.

HERR WEIRING: I do understand. I understand everything.

48

CHRISTINE: What?

HERR WEIRING: Go home.

CHRISTINE: Not till you tell me.

HERR WEIRING: I will tell you. It needs time.

CHRISTINE: I'll wait.

(*The* MUSICIANS, STAGE-HANDS, *etc.*, *have been progressively moving off stage and now* CHRISTINE *and* HERR WEIRING *are alone.*)

HERR WEIRING: Listen. The whole thing is a mistake. I've thought about it. You're so young.

CHRISTINE: Why are you saying this? What has changed?

HERR WEIRING: It's all wrong. It's delusion. Listen to me – it's best to forget all about it. It's just you and me again.

CHRISTINE: Stop talking like this. I confided in you. You can turn me out if you like but don't tell me it's a mistake –

HERR WEIRING: Turn you out? How can you say that? You only have me to protect you, and I failed you. We'll start again. You'll take singing lessons. There's a lot more to life. Being together. You and I. And summer's coming – we can go out to the country –

CHRISTINE: *What are you talking about?*

HERR WEIRING: *Listen*, damn you! You get more than one chance of happiness, don't you? You don't think everything stops the first time you get it or lose it?

CHRISTINE: Why should I have to lose it?

HERR WEIRING: And it was never happiness anyway – do you think that I don't know? It was misery.

CHRISTINE: You've heard something.

HERR WEIRING: No – nothing. But that man was playing with you, believe me, you've lost nothing. What do you know about him? Nothing. What did he know about your feelings? Did he appreciate you? Forget him. You'll meet someone decent, someone of your own kind and be happy. (*She breaks away.*)
Where are you going?

CHRISTINE: To find him. He can tell me himself.

WEIRING: Don't be stupid. He's not there –

CHRISTINE: I'll sit on his doorstep –

HERR WEIRING: I won't let you – for God's sake –

CHRISTINE: Then tell me what you know.

HERR WEIRING: What is there to know? I know that I love you, that you're my only child, that you belong with me – and I should never have let you –

CHRISTINE: That's enough! – Let go of me!

   (*They see that* THEODORE *has entered, with* MIZI *behind him.* THEODORE *is wearing his Dragoons uniform.*)

   Theo. . . ? What's happened? Where is he? Tell me.

THEODORE: Christine, he . . .

CHRISTINE: Tell me, can't you.

HERR WEIRING: He's dead.

CHRISTINE: (*Ignoring him*) Don't you dare say that, Theo. Tell me really.

HERR WEIRING: He's dead, my darling . . .

CHRISTINE: Theo . . .

   (THEODORE *nods.*)

THEODORE: Yes, he is.

CHRISTINE: For God's sake tell me, Theodore.

THEODORE: He's dead.

CHRISTINE: Yes. Of course he is. Don't touch me. Tell me.

THEODORE: What else is there to tell?

CHRISTINE: I don't know *anything*. I don't know what's happened.

THEODORE: It was an accident. Well, a sort of . . .

CHRISTINE: What? – Come on, Theo, do you think you have to spare me now? What difference does it make? How did it happen? Father. . . ? (*To* MIZI) You know, don't you?

MIZI: He was killed.

CHRISTINE: What do you mean he was. . . ?

THEODORE: He was killed in a duel.

CHRISTINE: Oh, my God –

   (HERR WEIRING *motions the others to leave.*)

Stay here. Do you think I'm not going to get it out of you.
Who killed him?

THEODORE: No one you know.

CHRISTINE: I know *that*, Theo. I know Frau Binder didn't kill
him – Damn you, Theo – I'm entitled to know – he loved me
and I have a right to know who killed him.

THEODORE: What does it matter? He fought a duel. A matter of
honour. He was killed.

CHRISTINE: Honour?

THEODORE: The usual thing. Well, what I mean is –

CHRISTINE: What you mean is what? A woman?

HERR WEIRING: Christine . . .

CHRISTINE: Of course. For a woman. (*To* MIZI) That woman in
the box. And her husband killed him. The usual thing. (*Cries
out.*) He died for *her*? He loved *her*?

THEODORE: Love? No, he was – it was just a madness.

CHRISTINE: Oh yes – mad about her, crazy for her, driven insane
by her. I know about that, it's what love is, Theo, didn't you
know that?

HERR WEIRING: Love isn't that – true love is something else,
you'll find out, Christine –

CHRISTINE: What was I, then?

MIZI: You were a bit of fun on the side, Chrissie, like me for
Theo –

THEODORE: I say, look –

CHRISTINE: Theodore, have you nothing for me? Didn't he write
anything for you to give me? A message? Nothing at all?
(THEODORE *shakes his head.*)
And when he came to see me that evening, he already knew.
He knew then that he probably wouldn't ever . . . He
amused himself with me and then went off to get himself
killed for the woman he loved. Didn't he know that I would
die for *him*?

THEODORE: (*Remembering with relief*) He spoke of you! He really
did. In the morning when we drove out together at dawn he
also spoke of you.

CHRISTINE: Also of me! Oh, good. He spoke of her, and him, and you, and his parents, his friends, and me.

THEODORE: I'm sure he loved you too.

CHRISTINE: Like you love Mizi? I worshipped him. He was God and salvation and I was his day off.

THEODORE: (*To* MIZI) Honestly, you could have spared me this – I've had enough upsets these last couple of days.
(*The* CONDUCTOR *and the* MUSICIANS *reappear, crossing the stage towards the pit.*)

CHRISTINE: Theodore, take me to him – I want to see him for the last time.

THEODORE: I can't –

CHRISTINE: Please – I want a proper last time, you can't deny me that.

THEODORE: It's too late. They buried him this morning.

CHRISTINE: Buried him? Without even telling me? They shot him and put him in a coffin and took him away and buried him and you didn't even tell me?

THEODORE: Listen, I haven't had a minute! These last two days, you've no idea . . . Don't forget I was the one who had to tell his parents, I had a lot on my mind, and consider my own feelings too, I was his best friend . . . and anyway it was all done very quietly, only the relatives and people closest to him –

CHRISTINE: Only the closest? And what am I, then?

MIZI: That's what they would have wanted to know.
(*The orchestra is heard tuning up. The* TENOR *and the* SOPRANO *return to the stage. The* TENOR *is wearing a different tunic. The* STAGE MANAGER *tries to get the attention of* HERR WEIRING, *indicating that the rehearsal must continue.*)

HERR WEIRING: (*To the* STAGE MANAGER) Yes . . . yes.

CHRISTINE: Take me to his grave.

HERR WEIRING: No, please – Christine –

STAGE MANAGER: (*Generally*) Please, ladies and gentlemen . . . Herr Weiring.

(HERR WEIRING *leaves down the steps, followed by the*
STAGE MANAGER.)

MIZI: Don't go, Christine – you may find *her* there, praying.

CHRISTINE: I'm not going there to pray.

THEODORE: Perhaps later when you're . . .

CHRISTINE: When I'm calmer?

THEODORE: Yes.

CHRISTINE: Tomorrow? Or in a month when I'm over it? Or
six months when I'm in love again? *Damn* you, Theo.

THEODORE: I'm very sorry. I thought you understood.
Everyone else did. How was I to know that . . .

CHRISTINE: What? That I loved him? You shit-bucket, Theo.
You fat, ugly, ignorant, lecherous, dirty-fingered God's gift
to the female race, your breath stank of stale women when
you kissed me, I was nearly *sick*!

(*The duet has now started again. The* TENOR *and the*
SOPRANO *are now singing together and alternately, and the
music and the dialogue are organized together so as to leave the
end of the chorus still to be sung after* CHRISTINE's *exit. The
last words of the play are thus the sung words:*)

Sweetheart, won't you dally, do
Or I'll die,
Or I'll die for love of you.

(CHRISTINE *leaves, pausing on her way to listen to the duet for
a few moments.* MIZI *and* THEODORE *remain, immobile
listening as the duet continues. Slow curtain.*)

UNDISCOVERED COUNTRY
Das weite Land
by Arthur Schnitzler

In an English version by
TOM STOPPARD

CHARACTERS

GENIA HOFREITER
FRIEDRICH HOFREITER, a businessman, Genia's husband
ERNA WAHL
DR FRANZ MAUER
MRS WAHL, Erna's mother
MRS MEINHOLD VON AIGNER, an actress, Otto's mother
ADELE NATTER
OTTO VON AIGNER, a lieutenant in the navy, Mrs von Aigner's son
DR VON AIGNER, divorced husband of Mrs von Aigner
PAUL KREINDL, a young man
MR NATTER, a banker, Adele's husband
ROSENSTOCK, porter of the Lake Vols Hotel
GUSTL WAHL, Mrs Wahl's son
MR SERKNITZ, a hotel guest
ALBERTUS RHON, a writer
PENN, a guide
MRS RHON, Albertus Rhon's wife
DEMETER STANZIDES, a captain in the Hussars
FIRST HIKER
SECOND HIKER
KATHI, the Hofreiters' maid
ITALIAN GIRL
SPANISH GIRL
FRENCH GIRL
BELLBOY
HEAD WAITER
THE NATTERS' TWO CHILDREN
FRENCH NANNY

Hotel guests, hikers, waiters

The action takes place at the Hofreiter villa in Baden, near Vienna, and at the Lake Vols Hotel in the Dolomites.

The first performance of *Undiscovered Country* was given at the Olivier Theatre, London, on 20 June 1979. The cast was as follows:

GENIA HOFREITER	Dorothy Tutin
FRIEDRICH HOFREITER	John Wood
ERNA WAHL	Emma Piper
DR FRANZ MAUER	Michael Byrne
MRS WAHL	Sara Kestelman
MRS MEINHOLD VON AIGNER	Joyce Redman
ADELE NATTER	Anna Carteret
OTTO VON AIGNER	Greg Hicks
DR VON AIGNER	Michael Bryant
PAUL KREINDL	John Harding
MR NATTER	Brian Kent
ROSENSTOCK	Peter Needham
GUSTL WAHL	Adam Norton
MR SERKNITZ	Roger Gartland
ALBERTUS RHON	Dermot Crowley
PENN	Martyn Whitby
MRS RHON	Marjorie Yates
DEMETER STANZIDES	Glyn Grain
FIRST HIKER	Elliott Cooper
SECOND HIKER	William Sleigh
KATHI	Janet Whiteside
ITALIAN GIRL	Susan Gilmore
SPANISH GIRL	Fiona Gaunt
FRENCH GIRL	Anne Sedgwick
BELLBOY	Mark Farmer
HEAD WAITER	Nik Forster
THE NATTERS' CHILDREN	{ Graham McGrath { Sandra Osborn
FRENCH NANNY	Marianne Morley
Directed by	Peter Wood
Designed by	William Dudley

ACT ONE

Conservatory and garden of the Hofreiter villa.
Late afternoon, after the rain.
GENIA HOFREITER, *dressed simply and respectably, stands listening*
to a Chopin record on the gramophone.
KATHI, *the maid, comes in with a tray to clear away the tea things,*
but hesitates.

KATHI: Shall I clear away, madam? Herr Hofreiter will no
doubt have taken tea in town.
(GENIA *nods, barely paying attention.*)
Shall I bring something to put round you, ma'am? It's
turned quite chilly.
GENIA: Mm . . .
(GENIA *notes the approach, beyond the fence and mostly hidden*
by it, of a funereal parasol and two elegant but equally funereal
head-dresses.)
. . . my white shawl.
(KATHI *completes her business and leaves with the tea things on*
her tray. MRS WAHL *and* ERNA *approach.* GENIA *waves her*
hand gracefully and moves to greet them. MRS WAHL, *slim and*
lively, about forty-five, has an air of self-conscious dignity. She
speaks through her nose in an aristocratic manner which is not
quite convincing. In expression and speech she is languid and
vivacious by turns. ERNA, *taller than her mother, slim;*
outspoken without being offensive; a cool, self-possessed
expression. GENIA *greets them, shaking hands.*)
Do come in. Safely back from town?
MRS WAHL: As you see, my dear Genia. The weather was
frightful.
GENIA: It rained out here, too, until an hour ago.
MRS WAHL: You did quite right to stay at home. We nearly
went under at the cemetery. It was only Erna made me go.

61

In my opinion, the church service would have been quite
sufficient. What good does it do anyone, after all?

ERNA: Mama is quite right there – we certainly didn't bring
poor Korsakow back to life.

GENIA: Many there?

MRS WAHL: *Tout le monde.* The Natters rolled up in their new
scarlet motor.

GENIA: (*Smiling*) It's seen all over the place, I hear.

MRS WAHL: Well, it certainly made a lively impression at the
cemetery . . .

(KATHI *comes out of the house with a white shawl, which she
puts around* GENIA.)

KATHI: Good evening, madam. Good evening, miss.

ERNA: Good evening.

MRS WAHL: (*Friendly*) Bless you, Kathi, dear . . .

(KATHI *exits.*)

GENIA: Did you speak to Friedrich out there?

MRS WAHL: Only in passing.

ERNA: He was quite upset.

GENIA: I'm not surprised.

ERNA: I was, as a matter of fact. He doesn't normally let things
affect him so easily.

GENIA: (*Smiling*) How well you seem to know him.

ERNA: Well, why not? (*Very simply*) I've loved him since I was
seven years old. I loved him before you did, Frau Genia.

GENIA: (*Chiding her affectionately*) Oh . . . *Frau* Genia, am I?

ERNA: (*Almost tenderly*) Genia.

(*She kisses* GENIA'*s hand.*)

GENIA: Friedrich was very fond of Alexei Korsakow, you know.

ERNA: Obviously. And there was I thinking that Korsakow was
just . . . his pianist.

GENIA: How do you mean, 'his pianist'?

ERNA: Well, just as Dr Mauer is his best friend, Mr Natter is
his banker, I'm his doubles partner, and Captain Stanzides
is his . . . his second . . .

GENIA: Oh . . .

ERNA: In theory, I mean . . . So I thought Korsakow was Friedrich's pianist. Friedrich takes from each according to his needs, you see . . .

MRS WAHL: Do you know, my dear Genia, what my late husband used to say about those remarks? – 'There goes Erna, pirouetting along the psychological tightrope.'

ERNA: Lieutenant!

(OTTO VON AIGNER *arrives at the edge of the garden.*)

OTTO: (*As he arrives*) Good evening.

GENIA: Good evening, Lieutenant von Aigner. Won't you come in for a moment?

OTTO: With your permission, ma'am.

(OTTO *enters the garden. He is a young man of twenty-five, modest and charming. He is wearing the uniform of a naval lieutenant.*)

GENIA: How is your mama? We haven't seen her today.

OTTO: Didn't she come yesterday, ma'am?

GENIA: Yes, she did. And the day before, too. (*Smiling*) You see she's been spoiling me.

OTTO: My mother has gone into town. She has a performance tonight. (*To* MRS WAHL *and* ERNA) I believe you ladies were also in town today. . . ?

MRS WAHL: We went to Korsakow's funeral.

OTTO: Of course . . . Does anybody have any idea why he killed himself?

ERNA: No.

MRS WAHL: Somebody at the funeral said they thought it was an artistic tantrum.

GENIA: What. . . ?

MRS WAHL: Yes. Because he was forever being told he could only play Chopin and Schumann, but not Beethoven or Bach . . . I must say I thought so too . . .

OTTO: Seems a bit extreme. Didn't he leave a note?

ERNA: Korsakow wouldn't be seen dead with a suicide note.

MRS WAHL: There she goes . . .

ERNA: He was far too intelligent and he had too much taste. He understood what it means to be dead, and so cared nothing for what people made of it next morning.

OTTO: I read in the papers that on the evening before he killed himself he was dining with friends . . . and was in excellent spirits . . .

MRS WAHL: The papers invariably say that.

GENIA: This time it happens to be true – my husband was one of the friends he dined with.

MRS WAHL: Ah . . .

GENIA: (*Casually*) When Friedrich has to work late in town he always dines at the Imperial Hotel. Korsakow was staying there. After dinner they went to the café and played billiards.

MRS WAHL: Just your husband and Korsakow?

GENIA: Yes. They even had a bet on – a box of cigars – and Friedrich lost. Next morning he sent Josef, his manservant, round from the flat with the cigars . . . and – didn't you know? – it was Josef who made the discovery.

MRS WAHL: What happened?

GENIA: Well, he knocked a few times – no reply; so finally he opened the door, and . . .

ERNA: There lay Korsakow, dead . . .

GENIA: Yes, with the revolver still in his hand . . .
(*Pause.*)

MRS WAHL: Awful moment for the manservant. What did he do with the cigars? Did he leave them?

ERNA: Mama believes in historical precision.
(*The sound of a car approaching.*)

MRS WAHL: It's stopping here.

GENIA: That's Friedrich's car.

ERNA: Good – we can arrange a game of tennis straight away. Is the court set up?

OTTO: Oh yes – Mr Hofreiter and I played singles for two hours yesterday.

MRS WAHL: You mean he was in the mood for tennis?

ERNA: Why shouldn't he be in the mood, Mama? When it's my

turn to go, people can knock up against my gravestone if they like.

(DR MAUER *arrives. He is thirty-five, with a blond full beard, pince-nez, sabre scar on his forehead; plainly, though not carelessly, dressed in a dark lounge suit.*)

MAUER: Good evening, dear friends.

GENIA: Oh, it's you, Doctor . . .

MAUER: (*Taking her hand, kissing it*) Greetings, dear lady. (*To* MRS WAHL) Good evening, Mrs Wahl. (*And to* ERNA) Ah . . . Miss Erna. Good evening, Lieutenant. (*To* GENIA) Friedrich presents his compliments, Frau Genia, but he's held up at the factory. He was kind enough to lend me his car to visit a couple of patients I've got out here. He's coming on by train.

MRS WAHL: Alas, we must go. (*To* MAUER) I hope we'll soon see you *chez nous*, Doctor. Although, thank God, we enjoy perfect health.

ERNA: You must come soon though, Doctor. We're off to the mountains in two weeks or so, to Lake Vols.

MAUER: Ah!

MRS WAHL: We're going to rendezvous with Gustl . . . (*To* OTTO) That's my wanderlust *Wunderkind* . . . He's been everywhere . . . India, last year.

ERNA: And I'm keen to go climbing again.

MAUER: Then there's a chance we'll meet up on some mountain peak. The fact is I'm also being drawn to the Dolomites. (*To* GENIA) And this year, dear Genia, I very much want to borrow Friedrich for the occasion.

MRS WAHL: I thought Friedrich had given up climbing since the accident . . .

MAUER: Not for ever, surely.

MRS WAHL: (*Explaining to* OTTO) Seven years ago a friend of Friedrich's, his name was Doctor Bernhaupt, crashed right past him on a rock-face . . .

ERNA: . . . and lay dead where he fell.

OTTO: (*To* GENIA) So it was your husband who was on that climb?

ERNA: (*Thoughtfully*) It has to be said, he doesn't have much luck with his friends.

GENIA: (*To* OTTO) You've heard about it, Mr von Aigner?

OTTO: Well, naturally . . . it happened on the Aignerturm . . . which my father was the first to climb more than twenty years ago.

GENIA: That's right, it was the Aignerturm.

MAUER: The Aignerturm . . . One quite forgets that it was named after a man who's still alive.
(*Short pause.*)

ERNA: Well, Lieutenant, it must be an extraordinary feeling to know that there is a mountain in the Dolomites to which you are, in a sense related.

OTTO: Not really, Fraulein. Both the mountain and my father are more or less strangers to me. I was a boy of four or five when my parents separated . . . and I haven't seen him since.
(*Pause.*)

ERNA: (*Encouraging her to leave*) Well, Mama . . .

MRS WAHL: Yes, indeed! If we're ever going to get unpacked . . . (*To* MAUER) We only moved out of town on Sunday. We haven't yet sat down to a proper meal . . . We have to eat in this awful park. Well, see you before long, Genia . . . (*To* OTTO) Will you come with us part of the way?

OTTO: If I may accompany you as far as the tennis courts . . . Goodbye, ma'am, please give my respects to your husband.

ERNA: Goodbye, Genia. *Auf Wiedersehen*, Doctor.
(*They take their leave.* GENIA *and* MAUER *remain.*)

MAUER: (*After a short pause, looking after* ERNA) Looking at the daughter, one could almost forgive the mother.

GENIA: A son-in-law could do a lot worse than Mrs Wahl . . . I should think it over, Doctor.

MAUER: (*Half joking*) I don't believe I cut enough of a dash for Erna.

GENIA: By the way, I had no idea that Friedrich was going to have to work late.

MAUER: Yes, I was meant to tell you, he had to wait for an important telegram, from America.

GENIA: Yes?

MAUER: Yes. Really. About that business of a patent for his latest invention, the incandescent light.

GENIA: (*Drily*) That was Edison.

(GENIA *sits down.*)

MAUER: Well, his improvement then. Anyway, as always, business seems to be booming. He's got a meeting with his banker first thing tomorrow.

GENIA: (*Slightly wary*) With Mr Natter?

MAUER: Natter *is* his banker.

GENIA: They were at the funeral too, I hear, the Natters.

MAUER: Yes.

GENIA: The scarlet motor car made an impression.

MAUER: (*Shrugs.*) So it's scarlet.

(*Short pause.* GENIA *watches* MAUER *with a faint smile.*)

By the way – your husband's affair with Mrs Natter is over.

GENIA: (*Still calm*) Oh really?

MAUER: Absolutely.

GENIA: That's good. Did Friedrich tell you?

MAUER: No, he wouldn't. But my diagnoses rarely call for a second opinion. In all honesty, there was never any cause to take it too seriously. Adele is very flighty.

GENIA: Oh yes, she's harmless. I'm not worried by her at all. But I think Mr Natter, for all his apparent friendliness, is a brutal man. Spiteful, too, in some ways. And sometimes I've been afraid for Friedrich; like a mother being worried about a son – a rather overgrown son – who's got himself into some scrape. You can understand what I mean?

MAUER: (*Sitting opposite her*) Yes, of course – the mark of a good wife, mothering her husband.

GENIA: I haven't always felt so. More than once I thought of leaving him.

MAUER: Oh!

GENIA: Once I even thought of killing myself. Mind you, that

was a long time ago. And perhaps it only seems like that to
me now . . .

MAUER: Quite so. You would never have done it . . . you
wouldn't have wished to cause him the inconvenience.

GENIA: Do you think I'm so considerate? You're quite wrong
. . . There was even a time when I thought of
inconveniencing Friedrich as only a wife can, especially a
wife with a possessive husband. I wanted revenge.

MAUER: Revenge?

GENIA: Well, let's say I wanted to get even.

MAUER: That would have been the rational thing to do. Well,
never mind . . . The fateful moment may still be waiting
for you, Frau Genia.

GENIA: I don't necessarily have to wait for it.

MAUER: (*Seriously*) But you will – alas. My sense of justice has
long been affronted by my old friend Friedrich getting off
scot-free.

GENIA: Oh, Friedrich pays. Not in the same coin, but he pays
all right. Sometimes I even feel sorry for him. Sometimes,
Doctor, I really think there's a demon driving him.

MAUER: A demon? Well, well! Even so, there are women we
know who would tell their husbands to go to hell and take
their demon with them.

(GENIA *looks at him inquiringly*.)

I was thinking of our local celebrity, Otto's mother.

GENIA: Mrs von Aigner?

MAUER: Yes, her husband was a bit of a devil with the ladies,
and she wasn't as resilient as you. Perhaps after all those
years in the theatre, real life took her by surprise.

GENIA: Perhaps she loved her husband more than I love
Friedrich. Perhaps the highest form of love leaves no room
for forgiveness.

(FRIEDRICH HOFREITER *enters. He is slim, with a thin,
distinguished face, a dark moustache clipped in the 'English'
style, blond hair, with the parting on the right and a touch of
grey. He wears pince-nez without a cord, and sometimes*

removes them. Tends to stoop a little. Small eyes, a little pinched. He speaks in a gentle, almost caressing way, which can change to biting sarcasm. His movements are graceful but suggest energy. He dresses elegantly but not foppishly: dark lounge suit, a black coat (not buttoned up) with wide satin lapels, a round black hat, a slim umbrella with a simple handle.)

FRIEDRICH: *(At the door)* Good evening. *(Coming in)* Hello, Mauer.

MAUER: *(Stands up.)* Hello there, Friedrich.

FRIEDRICH: *(Kisses* GENIA *lightly on the forehead.)* Good evening, Genia. How are you? Do you want to come to America?

GENIA: No. Do you want some tea?

FRIEDRICH: No . . . I had tea at the office. Pretty awful it was, too. Didn't Mauer tell you I was at the office?

GENIA: Yes . . . Did you get your telegram?

FRIEDRICH: I did . . . There are sailings to New York on August the 29th from Liverpool and on September the 2nd from Hamburg. North German Lloyd. The captain of the *King James* is a friend of mine.

GENIA: I expect we'll have another chance to talk about it before then.

FRIEDRICH: I hope to have that pleasure. I say, what a downpour that was. Did you have it out here? The cemetery was awash. But that was partly the speeches. An inch of slush fell in half an hour. You were well out of it . . . *(Pause.)* Well, Mauer, did the motor behave itself? How fast did you drive? Ten miles an hour, what? Safety first, that's you.

MAUER: Pull my leg if you like. I've had three cases of injury from car accidents in the last week.

FRIEDRICH: Oh yes – how *is* Stanzides?

MAUER: I'm just going to see him, as a matter of fact. He's very impatient, considering he ought to be grateful he didn't break his neck.

FRIEDRICH: Not to mention mine. I was thrown thirty feet up the road. But it's certainly true that the insurance companies will soon be turning down anyone who is acquainted with me.

MAUER: Yes, as Erna Wahl was saying, you're not very lucky with your friends.

FRIEDRICH: So Erna's been here?

GENIA: Yes, with her mother. They have just gone off with Otto.

FRIEDRICH: Otto too? (*To* MAUER) What did you think of him?

MAUER: (*Slightly surprised by the question*) A nice enough fellow.

FRIEDRICH: Remarkable how like his father he is.

MAUER: Is he? . . . Dr von Aigner was never my type, as a matter of fact. Had too many affectations.

FRIEDRICH: What he had was style. They're often confused. It's a long time, too, since I saw him. Do you remember, Genia?

GENIA: Oh yes. (*To* MAUER) I liked him very much.

FRIEDRICH: Yes, he was in fine fettle then. That's more than I was. (*To* MAUER) It was just a few days after the Bernhaupt thing. Yes, and Aigner had just come back from an election campaign. They say he's got at least one child in every village in the Tyrol. And not just in his own constituency either.

MAUER: All right then, let's call it style. But I really must be going now. Stanzides will be expecting me.

FRIEDRICH: You will come back here for supper afterwards?

MAUER: I don't know.

FRIEDRICH: Of course you will.

MAUER: (*Hesitatingly*) Thank you. But I must catch the 10.20 back to town. I have to be early at the hospital.

FRIEDRICH: Are you superstitious, Mauer?

MAUER: Why?

FRIEDRICH: I thought perhaps you didn't want to spend the night in our guest room since poor Korsakow slept there a week ago. But I don't think the dead are allowed out round their old haunts on their very first night.

MAUER: How can you talk like that?

FRIEDRICH: (*Suddenly serious*) You're right, it's really awful. A week ago he slept up there, and the evening before that he played the piano in there . . . Chopin – the Nocturne in C sharp minor – and something by Schumann . . . and we sat on the veranda there, Otto was here too, and the Natters . . . who would have dreamed. . . ! If only one had an idea why . . . Genia – didn't he say anything to you either?

GENIA: Me?

MAUER: (*Helping out*) Well, artists are all more or less unhinged, aren't they? For one thing, the way they take themselves so seriously. Ambition is a disturbance of the balance of the mind. All that banking on immortality. . . !

FRIEDRICH: What are you talking about! You didn't even know him. None of you knew him. Ambitious . . . Korsakow? No, he'd got that handsome head screwed on all right. Bashing the ivories was just something to do. Do you know what he was really interested in? He had Kant and Schopenhauer and Nietzsche at his fingertips, and Marx and Proudhon . . . He was amazing. And twenty-seven years old!! And kills himself. Dear God, a fellow like that, with so much before him! Young and famous, and with that profile, too . . . and he shoots himself. If it was some old ass, for whom life had nothing more to offer . . . And the evening before, there we were sitting down to supper with a man like that . . . playing billiards with him . . . What is it, Genia? What is there to laugh at?

GENIA: Mrs Wahl wanted to know what became of the cigars.

FRIEDRICH: Ha! . . . She's really priceless. (*Takes a box of cigars from his pocket, offers them to* MAUER.) Josef brought them back to me, of course. Go on, have one. Korsakow has given them up.

MAUER: Thank you. One shouldn't really, just before supper. (*He takes one.* FRIEDRICH *lights it for him.* KATHI *enters with letters.* GENIA *takes them from her.*)

GENIA: Postcard from Joey.

FRIEDRICH: 'Dear Mother'. For you. Just a postcard, once again. Lazy devil.

MAUER: Well, I'll be off. I'll be back in half an hour. By the way, this cigar is just about ready to join Korsakow, and that's no superstition. Don't get up.
(*He leaves.*)

FRIEDRICH: Yes, it was just as well that you didn't go, Genia. Between the drizzle and the drivel . . . (*He flicks through the letters and the newspapers.*) . . . oh yes, as the coffin disappeared the sun suddenly came out. (*Pause.*) Isn't it Thursday today? He was going to have supper with us today. Here, let's have a look at Joey's card.

GENIA: (*Passes it to him.*) He'll be here in four weeks.

FRIEDRICH: (*Reading it*) Yes. Hm . . . top in Greek. Well, not too bad. Perhaps he'll be a philologist, or an archaeologist. By the way, did you see the article in yesterday's London *Times* about the latest excavations in Crete?

GENIA: No.

FRIEDRICH: Very interesting.

GENIA: Why? Did they dig up a light bulb? (*Pause.*) What was that about America – were you serious?

FRIEDRICH: Of course. Well, wouldn't you like to, Genia?
(GENIA *slowly shakes her head.*)

GENIA: But I was thinking, while you're over there, I thought I'd go to England – stay with Joey.

FRIEDRICH: Where did this notion suddenly come from?

GENIA: It's not so sudden. And since you seem determined to let him stay over there for years to come . . .

FRIEDRICH: Well, you can see how famously he's getting on. It would be damned selfish to interrupt all that fagging and cricket and bring him back here where they educate you in every kind of sentimental brutality.

GENIA: If it wasn't for missing him so . . .

FRIEDRICH: Yes, of course . . . I suppose you think I don't yearn for him? But in my opinion, yearning is a necessary part of the soul's economy. Relationships are all the better for it. In an ideal world more and more people would see less and less of each other. Anyway we can go back with Joey to England, and you can decide then if you want to come with me or stay with the boy through the winter.

GENIA: I'd rather you took it as final.

FRIEDRICH: Final? Look, what's the matter with you, Genia? You're behaving very oddly.

GENIA: What's so odd about it? . . . Soon he won't be mine any more. It's not enough – two months in the summer, a week at Christmas and Easter – I've borne it long enough – I can't go on any longer!

(GENIA *moves into the garden.* FRIEDRICH *looks after her.* GENIA *walks along the lawn, moving upstage.* FRIEDRICH *follows her. He pauses by a rose bush. He smells a flower.*)

FRIEDRICH: The roses have no scent at all this year. I don't know why it is. Every year they look more gorgeous, but they've stopped bothering. Genia . . .

GENIA: What?

FRIEDRICH: No, I'll wait till you get here. Tell me something. (*Looking her in the eye, quite calmly*) I was wondering whether perhaps *you* knew why Korsakow shot himself. . . ?

GENIA: (*Calmly*) You know I was just as surprised as you were.

FRIEDRICH: That's the impression one got, of course. Well, tell me why you want to leave me . . . at a moment's notice.

GENIA: I don't want to leave you. I want to visit Joey. And not at a moment's notice, but in the autumn. To be with Joey.

FRIEDRICH: Yes, otherwise it would almost look as if you were running away.

GENIA: I'm under no such necessity – we could hardly be further apart than we are.

FRIEDRICH: Look, Genia! He's dead and buried – Herr Alexei Korsakow.

GENIA: Then I suggest you stop digging him up!

FRIEDRICH: Don't get excited, my love, calm at all costs . . . I'm only trying to say that it can't make the slightest difference to him now if you . . . not that anything would happen to him if

he were still alive, of course . . . no more than to you . . .
Don't misunderstand me, Genia. Nothing much need have
happened between you. It could have been just a flirtation.
Yes. Because if there had been anything more to it – why
shoot himself? Unless (*seizing on it*) there *was* more to it –
and you . . . ended it.

(*He has been speaking quite quietly but now takes her arm.*)

GENIA: (*Almost amused*) A jealous scene? Really! . . . You ought
to take something for your nerves, Friedrich, I don't know
. . . but I can't help it if Adele Natter is finished with you
and you haven't yet found a replacement.

FRIEDRICH: Ah, you are very well informed. Well, I won't
inquire as to the source of that knowledge. Besides, it's not
my fault that you never asked me straight out – I wouldn't
have told you you ought to take something for your nerves.
That isn't like you at all. I really don't understand you. It's
as though you didn't trust me, Genia. But I promise you,
Genia – don't think I'm being devious – I would understand
completely. You can't imagine how unimportant certain
things become when you have just left a cemetery. So come
– tell me. You can lie if you want, but answer you must. If
it's true I'll find out anyway. Well . . . yes or no?

GENIA: He was not my lover. Unfortunately, he was not my
lover. Does that satisfy you?

FRIEDRICH: Perfectly! So you were lovers. Well, if you say
'unfortunately', ergo you loved him and because you loved
him, naturally you . . . What was there to stop you? And
when you – put an end to it, he killed himself. And I can
tell you why you put an end to it, too. Firstly because these
things have to come to an end anyway. Especially in the
case of a younger man – who is usually away on some
concert tour. And then Joey's coming back soon, and when
he does you'd like to feel – how shall I put it? – unsullied
. . . Well . . . all very respectable. All very clear so far.
Except for this idea about a trip to England. No, come to
that, that makes sense too.

GENIA: Friedrich! Read that.
(*She takes a letter from her belt.*)
FRIEDRICH: What do you want me to. . . ?
GENIA: Read it.
FRIEDRICH: What is it . . . a letter? A letter from him? Ah, keep it. I don't want it.
GENIA: I said read it!
FRIEDRICH: Anyway, why should I have to? You can tell me what's in it. It could well be in Russian . . . and tiny handwriting. One could do irreparable damage to one's eyesight.
GENIA: Read it.
(FRIEDRICH *turns the wall light on, sits under it, puts on his pince-nez and begins to read.*)
FRIEDRICH: (*Reading*) 'Farewell, Genia.' (*Looks up at her, in astonishment.*) When did you get the letter, then?
GENIA: An hour before you brought the news of his death.
FRIEDRICH: So when I came home, you already knew. . . ? I'm just . . . Well, at the risk of your thinking me a complete idiot, I didn't notice a thing, not a thing . . . (*Reads to himself for a while, then looks at her in surprise again, then reads half to himself.*) 'Perhaps it was as well you rejected my presumptuous advances. Neither of us was made for deceit . . . I was, perhaps, but not you . . . in spite of everything . . .' In spite of everything . . . You must have complained about me a good deal. (*Reading*) 'Now I do understand why, in spite of everything, you don't want to leave Him . . .' With a capital H, very flattering. 'You love him, Genia, you still love your husband, the mystery is resolved. And perhaps what I refer to by that stupid word . . .' I can't read this bit at all . . .
GENIA: 'That stupid word faithfulness . . .'
FRIEDRICH: Thank you . . . 'is nothing more than the hope that he will one day come back to you.'
GENIA: That's his interpretation. You know I hope for nothing – and want nothing.

FRIEDRICH: (*Looks at her. Then –*) 'When I spoke to you
yesterday I had already made up my mind . . .' Yesterday?
. . . Was he here on Sunday then? Yes, that's right, you
were walking up and down the path together, back there
. . . yes . . . (*Reading*) 'When I spoke to you yesterday I
had already made up my mind that everything would
depend on your yes or no. I have told you nothing about it
because I was afraid that if you had suspected that I just
couldn't go on living without you . . .' He writes in
considerable detail, does Herr Alexei Ivanovitsch . . .
Would you have said yes if you had known it was a matter
of life or death?

GENIA: If I had *known*. . . ? Could one ever. . . ?

FRIEDRICH: Well, let me put it another way . . . though it's six
of one and . . .

(PAUL KREINDL, *elegant, young, dreadfully smart, appears at
the gate, interrupting* FRIEDRICH.)

PAUL: Good evening!

FRIEDRICH: Whom have we here?

PAUL: My compliments, ma'am.

FRIEDRICH: . . . Ah, Paul, it's you.

(*He comes down from the veranda.*)

PAUL: Forgive me. (*He approaches* FRIEDRICH.) Don't let me
disturb you. The thing is, I've come as an ambassador from
the park – from Mrs Wahl and Miss Erna and Lieutenant
von Aigner and Captain Stanzides . . .

FRIEDRICH: He's abroad already?

PAUL: Would the present company care to come to the concert?

GENIA: I'm afraid we have a guest for supper – Dr Mauer.

PAUL: Well, do bring him along too, ma'am!

FRIEDRICH: All right then – perhaps we'll come on later . . .
but no promises.

GENIA: Thank you all the same.

PAUL: Oh, not at all. We would all be delightd. I take my leave,
ma'am. Adieu, Mr Hofreiter. A thousand pardons for
disturbing you.

(*He exits. Pause.*)

FRIEDRICH: . . . and half a dozen of the other, but I'll put it another way. I mean, suppose you could bring him back to life by telling him you were prepared . . . to be his mistress.

GENIA: I don't know.

FRIEDRICH: You can't have been that far from it . . . Come on, you *did* love him . . .

GENIA: But not enough, as you see.

FRIEDRICH: You say that as if it was *my* fault.

GENIA: No. It was mine.

FRIEDRICH: But you do reproach yourself that you . . . drove him to kill himself.

GENIA: I'm sorry he's dead. But what should I reproach myself for? – my faithfulness?
(*Pause.*)

FRIEDRICH: Here's your letter, Genia.
(GENIA *takes the letter as* MAUER *arrives.*)

MAUER: Here we are again . . . I hope I haven't kept you from supper?

GENIA: I'll go and see how it's getting on . . .

FRIEDRICH: Look, I've got an idea . . . Let's go to the park right away. I'm damned if I'm not in the mood for music and company. It's all the same to you, Mauer, isn't it?

MAUER: Me? What about your wife?

GENIA: (*Reluctantly*) I'd have to change . . .

FRIEDRICH: Hurry up and change then, we'll be waiting for you in the garden. (*To* MAUER) What do you say? (*Nervily*) All right then, let's stay at home then, fine . . . that's an end of it.

GENIA: I'll be right back . . . I'll just put my hat on.
(*She exits. Pause.*)

MAUER: I really don't understand you . . .

FRIEDRICH: Oh, nothing wrong with the park, you can get a good meal there. (*Pause.*) By the way – it's probably just as well that you're not stopping the night. The chances of a ghostly apparition in this house have considerably increased.

MAUER: What?

FRIEDRICH: Actually, you don't deserve my confidence, you blurt out everything you know, even things I never told you . . .

MAUER: What do you mean?

FRIEDRICH: Well, how did Genia find out that I've finished my affair with Adele Natter?

MAUER: You ought to be thankful that for once it is possible to say something to your credit . . . What was that about a ghost?

FRIEDRICH: What. . . ? Oh, that – Well, why do you think Korsakow killed himself? Go on, have a guess! – Because of a hopeless love – for my wife. Yes. A hopeless love! Now we know there is such a thing . . . He left a letter for her. She made me read it . . . quite a remarkable letter . . . not at all badly written . . . for a Russian.

(GENIA *comes in with her hat on. The music from the park can be heard.*)

GENIA: Here I am. Well, dear Doctor, let me tell you that it's only for your sake that I've abandoned our nice supper. Erna is in the park.

FRIEDRICH: Ah? Erna! (*To* MAUER) Yes, that would be quite a match. Well, dear chap, gird yourself. I wouldn't let anybody have her.

(*They all leave the garden.*)

ACT TWO

The Hofreiter villa. Another part of the garden. The back of the house, with doors opening directly on to the garden. A small balcony on the first floor. A tree, a bench, table and chair. A partly obscured tennis court in the background, with wire netting around it. A hot, sunny, summer's day.

GENIA *is sitting in the garden, in a white dress, a book in her hand, but she is not reading. On the tennis court a game in progress, involving* FRIEDRICH, ADELE, ERNA *and* PAUL. *One may see the bright white tennis clothes but not much of the people. From time to time one can hear the sounds of tennis.*

OTTO VON AIGNER *arrives, wearing tennis clothes with a panama hat, and carrying a tennis racket. He is on his way to the tennis court, but catches sight of* GENIA. *He goes up to her. She greets him with a friendly nod.*

OTTO: Good morning, ma'am – you're not playing?
GENIA: As you see, Lieutenant. I'm no match for that
 company.
OTTO: They're not all athletes either . . . I don't speak for your
 husband, of course. I mean . . . (*Pause.*) . . . Forgive me,
 ma'am, I'm disturbing your reading.
GENIA: You aren't disturbing me at all. We haven't seen your
 mother. Does she have a performance today?
OTTO: Oh, no.
GENIA: It must be nice for your mother to have you with her
 again.
OTTO: And for me . . . Especially since this is my last leave for
 some time to come. I've been ordered to a ship that's going
 to the South Seas for three years.
GENIA: (*Conventionally*) Oh.
OTTO: The War Ministry has attached us to a scientific
 expedition.

79

GENIA: The South Seas. . . ? I dare say you will fill up your free
time with all kinds of studies, eh, Lieutenant?

OTTO: How do you mean, ma'am?

GENIA: I wouldn't imagine that official duties cover all your
interests?

OTTO: (*Smiling*) Permit me to observe that in the navy we
undertake all sorts of things which could, without
presumption, be described as showing the flag.

GENIA: That's what I thought.

OTTO: Actually, I hope to learn more about a subject which up
to now I have studied only superficially . . . Our expedition
is equipped for deep-sea exploration, and one of the
technicians . . .

(MRS WAHL *approaches*.)

GENIA: (*Rising*) You must tell me more another time,
Lieutenant . . . about these deep waters . . .

MRS WAHL: Good day to you, Genia. Good day, Lieutenant.
(*She puts her lorgnette to her eyes to look at the tennis court*.)
The young generation already hard at play. . . ?

GENIA: If you include Friedrich.

MRS WAHL: Friedrich especially. Who's still playing, then?
Adele Natter, for one . . . I saw the scarlet motor car
outside. It doesn't look so out of place in the country –
compared with the cemetery.

GENIA: (*Smiling faintly*) It seems to have made a lasting
impression on you.

MRS WAHL: Well, it's only a fortnight . . .
(FRIEDRICH *and* ERNA *come from the court with their rackets
in their hands*.)

FRIEDRICH: (*In his laughing, mischievous mood*) What's only a
fortnight? How are you, Mama Wahl? Hello there, Otto!

MRS WAHL: Poor Korsakow's funeral.

FRIEDRICH: Oh yes . . . Was it as long ago as that? How did
you get on to this black-bordered subject, anyway?

GENIA: Mrs von Wahl saw the Natters' motor car outside – the
scarlet one – it reminded her.

FRIEDRICH: Ah ha –

ERNA: Who else would go from a scarlet motor to a dead piano player on such a beautiful summer's day?

MRS WAHL: Did you ever see such a deep-thinking girl? Another of her performances on the philosophical flying-trapeze, as her late father used to say.

ERNA: No, he didn't.

MRS WAHL: Must have been someone else.

FRIEDRICH: She'd best take care she doesn't fall off one fine day, our little Erna . . .

(ADELE NATTER *and* PAUL KREINDL *come from the tennis court with their rackets. General greetings. Adele is pretty, plump, wearing white with red belt and floating red scarf.*)

ADELE: What's happening then, aren't we going to play any more?

(PAUL *kisses* MRS WAHL's *hand.*)

FRIEDRICH: You could have carried on with singles.

ADELE: But I play too badly for this gentleman here.

PAUL: What do you mean, ma'am? (*Whining*) I'll soon have no one bad enough to play with me. Honestly I've been playing like a pregnant sow. Pardon me, but honestly it's true. It's exactly as though I'd been put under a spell. Or perhaps it's just that I've got a new racket. Would the distinguished company excuse me – I'm going to rush off home and get my old one.

(*He takes his leave to general laughter.*)

FRIEDRICH: What is there to laugh at? He at least takes it seriously. In my opinion a good tennis player is a nobler specimen of humanity than a mediocre poet or general. (*To* OTTO) Well, aren't I right?

ADELE: (*To* GENIA) Well now, when is Master Joey returning, Frau Genia?

GENIA: In a fortnight. And then you must bring your children along one day, won't you?

ADELE: Gladly, if you'd let me. Although whether your big boy will deign to play with my little rascals . . .

(DR MAUER *arrives, with* STANZIDES *in uniform.*)

STANZIDES: My compliments!

GENIA: (*To* STANZIDES) Ah, Stanzides, it's nice to have you with us again.

FRIEDRICH: How's the arm?

STANZIDES: Thanks for asking. My medical adviser has just given it a final prod. But I still can't play tennis yet.

MAUER: But you will.

STANZIDES: (*To* ADELE) Are you ready for the fray too, ma'am? I just had the pleasure of meeting your husband in the park.

FRIEDRICH: Now, Mauer – you've been keeping yourself well out of sight. I thought you were already over the hills and far away.

MAUER: I leave tomorrow.

GENIA: Where are you going?

MAUER: To Toblach. From there I'll walk the passes – Falzárego, Pordio . . .

FRIEDRICH: Will you take me with you, Mauer?

MAUER: Can you? And do you really want to?

FRIEDRICH: Yes – why not? . . . You start tomorrow?

MAUER: First thing, I'm taking the express.

ERNA: (*To* MAUER) And when will we have the pleasure of welcoming you to Lake Vols?

MAUER: In a week or so, if that's all right.

FRIEDRICH: (*Frankly put out*) Ah . . . everyone planning their assignations . . .

ERNA: And without asking your permission, Friedrich!

MRS WAHL: We're going the day after tomorrow – straight to Lake Vols.

(*During the following,* OTTO, GENIA *and* ADELE *form a group to one side.*)

My Gustl is already there. By the way, the things he's been telling me about in his letters . . . Do you know who the manager of the new hotel is? Otto's father, Dr von Aigner.

FRIEDRICH: Oh . . . Aigner!

MRS WAHL: And apparently all the ladies are in a spin over him, despite his grey hair.

FRIEDRICH: Yes, women have always been putty in his hands. So have a care, Mama Wahl.

PAUL: (*Returning*) Back again! (*Holding his racket up*) There's my old beauty! Now I feel I've got something I can volley with.

FRIEDRICH: Well, shall we start? (*To* PAUL) But no more excuses! Or change your vocation – take up some local pastime – light opera – or psychoanalysis . . .
   (FRIEDRICH, OTTO, ERNA, ADELE *and* PAUL *go to play tennis.* MRS WAHL *and* STANZIDES *follow.* GENIA *and* MAUER *remain.*)

GENIA: Shall we watch the game? Erna's particularly worth watching on the tennis court!

MAUER: Can't you see, my dear friend, that she doesn't care two pins for me?

GENIA: Perhaps that's the best foundation for a happy marriage.

MAUER: Oh yes, if I reciprocated her feelings, but in this case . . . (*Breaking off*) By the way, Frau Genia, is Friedrich serious about coming with me?

GENIA: I don't know. I was taken by surprise myself.

MAUER: What about this American trip?

GENIA: Friedrich is going over.

MAUER: And you?

GENIA: I might.

MAUER: You'll be travelling together. Bravo.

GENIA: Spare the celebration . . . I said I might.

MAUER: But you'll go. It would really be too silly for Korsakow to have died entirely in vain. Yes, I'm convinced that Korsakow was destined by providence to . . . fall as a sacrifice.

GENIA: (*Increasingly bewildered*) As a sacrifice?

MAUER: For you – and your happiness.

GENIA: You believe in that sort of thing?

MAUER: Generally speaking I don't, but in this case I feel

something of the mysterious connection between things. Hasn't the same thought occurred to you?

GENIA: Me? I confess I forget to think about that sad business. I feel a slight pang – nothing more. Is there no way I can be better or less insensitive than I am? Perhaps I'll feel differently later. Perhaps when autumn comes. Perhaps the days are too bright and summery for sorrow – or indeed for taking anything too seriously. For instance, I can't even be angry with Adele Natter. It just seems pointless to bear her a grudge.

MAUER: Well, now at last things will change between you. One can't stay angry with old Friedrich for long. I'm just the same where he's concerned. I may get absolutely furious with him – but as soon as he turns on the charm, I'm at his mercy again.

(KATHI *enters from the house.*)

GENIA: Well, I'm not! I need to be wooed – long and patiently.

(OTTO, FRIEDRICH, ADELE, STANZIDES *and* MRS WAHL *come from the court.*)

(*Having received a word from* KATHI) If you're ready, ladies and gentlemen . . . Tea! Ice-cream is available too. No one need feel obliged . . .

(MRS WAHL *and* STANZIDES, GENIA *and* OTTO, *and* MAUER *go into the house.* FRIEDRICH *and* ADELE *remain behind.*)

FRIEDRICH: (*As* ADELE *is about to go into the house*) I'm afraid, Mrs Natter, I haven't yet had the opportunity to inquire after your health. How are you then, Addy?

ADELE: I'm extremely well, Mr Hofreiter. And may I suggest that you address me with a little less familiarity? What's over is over. I like straightforward relationships.

FRIEDRICH: Really? – I had the impression you like ambiguous ones.

ADELE: Don't. We should be glad that it ended without mishap. We're both of us too old for youthful follies. My children are growing up. And your boy, too.

FRIEDRICH: What difference does that make?

ADELE: And if you would allow me to give you some advice, I think the way you're flirting with Mrs Wahl's little girl is frankly disgraceful. And for heaven's sake don't think this is jealousy. I'm not thinking of you at all . . . more of your wife . . .

FRIEDRICH: (*Amused*) Ah!

ADELE: . . . who really is the sweetest, most touching creature I've ever met. When she asked me to bring the children round – did you hear her? – I wanted the earth to swallow me up!

FRIEDRICH: I assure you it didn't show.

ADELE: Truly, you don't deserve her.

FRIEDRICH: I can't say you're wrong about that. But I can't imagine what you're suggesting. Erna! A girl I have dandled on my knee.

ADELE: What difference does that make? There are girls of all ages of whom that can be said.

FRIEDRICH: Very true, Adele. It's not a bad idea . . . oh, Addy, it would be wonderful to be young again!

ADELE: You've been young quite long enough.

FRIEDRICH: Yes, but I was young too soon . . . these things are so badly arranged. One ought to be young at forty, then you'd get something out of it. Shall I tell you something, Adele? It really does seem to me that everything that has happened up to now has only been a preparation. And that now life and love are just beginning.

ADELE: There is more to life than – women to make love to.

FRIEDRICH: Oh, yes – there are the spaces between them. Not uninteresting. If one has the time and if one is in the mood, one builds factories, conquers nations, writes symphonies, becomes a millionaire . . . but, believe me, all that is merely to fill in the time. Life is for you! for you, for you! . . .

ADELE: (*Shaking her head*) And to think that there are people who take you seriously!

(MR NATTER *arrives. A tall, rather robust man, in a very elegant summer suit: mutton-chop whiskers, and monocle.*)

85

NATTER: Good evening, Adele! How are you, Hofreiter, old man?

FRIEDRICH: (*Extending his hand*) Natter! Why are you so late?

ADELE: (*Very affectionately*) So, what have you been up to?

NATTER: Forgive me, my love. I've been sitting in the park reading – it's the only chance I get. Tell me, Hofreiter, is there anything nicer than sitting under a tree with a book?

FRIEDRICH: That depends . . . on the book . . .

(PAUL *and* ERNA *come from the court.* MAUER *comes out of the house.*)

PAUL: Honestly, Miss Erna, true as I stand here! Your service – absolutely terrific!

FRIEDRICH: Yes – and what about her backhand return? She learned that from me, too.

ERNA: A dubious boast.

FRIEDRICH: See what I mean?

ERNA: (*To the others, especially* PAUL) He was merciless! And at the first sign of slacking off one was treated like a miserable sinner . . .

FRIEDRICH: (*Casually*) Yes – these things are all a matter of character, in my opinion . . . (*To* NATTER) Will you have some tea with us? We were just about to . . .

NATTER: Love to . . . By the way, is Stanzides still here?

FRIEDRICH: Oh, bound to be.

NATTER: I want to ask him to come to the theatre with us. (*To* ADELE) If that's all right with you. I've taken a box in the Arena.

(MAUER *and* ERNA *have moved to one side.*)

FRIEDRICH: Does that trash amuse you?

NATTER: And why not?

ADELE: There's nothing on earth that doesn't amuse him. My husband is the best audience anyone could have.

NATTER: Yes, that's true. I find life entirely amusing.

(FRIEDRICH, ADELE *and* NATTER *enter the house.* MAUER *and* ERNA *are already in conversation.*)

MAUER: Shall I come, then?

ERNA: Of course you must. I'll engage you as our guide, for the usual fee, naturally.

MAUER: I never imagined that I could lay claim to anything more.

ERNA: Was that in earnest, Dr Mauer, or in jest?

MAUER: Shall I come to Lake Vols, Fraulein Erna, yes or no?

ERNA: I can see no reason at all why you should alter your plans.

MAUER: Is it really impossible for you to give me a straight answer, Erna?

ERNA: It's not easy, Doctor. You know I'm very fond of you. You ought to come anyway. It would be the best way for us to get to know one another better. But naturally, you mustn't feel any more committed than I do.

MAUER: Neatly spoken.

ERNA: And there's more. Listen. Naturally you have a favourite ladyfriend or some such – all unmarried gentlemen have. Well, don't be hasty. I mean, don't go away after our conversation thinking that you owe me your faithfulness.

MAUER: Alas, your kind concern comes too late. Of course, I can't deny that, like all men, as you say . . . but not any longer . . . in my case. A squalid affair has no appeal to me. I would disgust myself.

ERNA: What a gentleman you are, Dr Mauer! I feel that if one put one's fate in your hands . . . one would have reached harbour.

MAUER: Don't think me a fool, Miss Erna, if I venture that at my side you may find, if not perhaps the best that life can offer, at least much that is worthwhile.

ERNA: To be frank, Dr Mauer, I sometimes feel that I need something more from life than security and peace.

MAUER: There is more to life than adventure . . . Well, shall I say, adventures of a certain kind.

ERNA: Have I suggested. . . ?

MAUER: You haven't said so, Miss Erna, but that's what you are thinking. And who's to wonder – in the very air we breathe!

87

But I tell you, I could show you another world – where the air is purer.

ERNA: You're not a fool, Doctor. I like your frankness. I like you very much. Come to Lake Vols. We'll see.

(ADELE, NATTER *and* STANZIDES *come out of the house, followed at intervals by* GENIA, OTTO, PAUL, FRIEDRICH *and* MRS WAHL.)

STANZIDES: Sometimes in the old days I didn't watch the show from the auditorium at all, but from way above – a bird's-eye view from the hill behind the Arena.

ADELE: That must be fun.

STANZIDES: I don't know about fun. It's certainly strange. You can only see a little bit of the stage-setting, of course. A corner of a crag, or a statue, or something. And of course you see nothing at all of the actors, you just hear the odd word every now and then . . . but the strangest thing is when without warning, among all those voices, one floats up to you and you recognize it – for example if you happen to be a friend of one of the actresses. And then all of a sudden you can understand the words too. Nothing of what the others are saying – only the familiar voice of the actress with whom you have been friends.

ADELE: (*Laughing*) Or the friendly voice of the actress with whom you have been familiar!

FRIEDRICH: To speak of being familiar with a loved one is a contradiction in terms . . . Lovers should be referred to as constant unfamiliars . . .

ADELE: Or members of the fair sex, if you're being discreet.

FRIEDRICH: Or unfair sex.

ERNA: If you're not.

MRS WAHL: Erna!

NATTER: It's getting late. We must be going if we want to see anything of the show. Please don't let us disturb you.

(NATTER, ADELE *and* STANZIDES *leave*.)

PAUL: (*To* OTTO) Once – last year – Dr Herz and I took a set to 28 games to 26. After the first four hours we had an omelette . . .

OTTO: What sort of omelette?

(*He continues listening to* PAUL.)

MAUER: Time for me as well . . . (*To* GENIA) Dear lady . . .

FRIEDRICH: Look, why be in such a hurry? Give me a quarter of an hour and I'll drive in with you.

MAUER: What – are you serious then?

FRIEDRICH: Of course . . . you'll wait then?

GENIA: You mean you're going into town with Dr Mauer? Now?

FRIEDRICH: Yes, that's the most sensible thing. I've got all the things I need for the mountains at the flat. Josef can pack them for me in an hour, then I'll be able to set off with Mauer first thing in the morning.

MAUER: All right.

GENIA: But . . .

FRIEDRICH: So you'll wait? – Fifteen minutes.

MAUER: Yes, I'll wait.

(FRIEDRICH *goes quickly into the house.* ERNA, PAUL, OTTO *and* MRS WAHL *are standing together.* GENIA's *gaze follows* FRIEDRICH.)

PAUL: Come on, then, let's not waste the last of the light . . .

MAUER: (*To* GENIA) He's a man of quick decisions.

(GENIA *doesn't reply.* ERNA, OTTO, PAUL *and* MRS WAHL *move off towards the tennis court.* MAUER *follows after a brief pause.* GENIA *still stands motionless, then moves suddenly to go into the house, but meets* MRS VON AIGNER *coming out.* MRS VON AIGNER *is about forty-four, and looks it, her features being somewhat worn, though her figure is still youthful.*)

MRS VON AIGNER: Good evening.

GENIA: Oh, Mrs von Aigner, so late? I was afraid you weren't going to come at all today. Now I'm doubly happy that you're here. Come, won't you sit down, dear Mrs von Aigner? Perhaps over there – it's your favourite spot.

MRS VON AIGNER: (*Noticing* GENIA's *distracted air*) Thank you, thank you.

GENIA: Or shall we go to the tennis court? They're playing heart and soul over there, and you enjoy watching Otto, don't you?

MRS VON AIGNER: (*Smiling*) But it's not Otto I've come to see, I've come to see you, dear Mrs Hofreiter. Only aren't I disturbing you? You seem to me a little . . . perhaps you'd rather go into the house?

GENIA: Not at all. It's just that . . . my husband is going to town with Dr Mauer. Actually, he's going away with him tomorrow. They're going on a walking holiday together. Just imagine, an hour ago he didn't know himself. And now he's just off.

(*She looks up at the balcony.*)

MRS VON AIGNER: Then I've certainly come at a bad time for you.

GENIA: Oh no, it's not for long. We're not sentimental about being parted, believe me.

MRS VON AIGNER: Yes, I see. But what about Joey – won't he be back soon?

GENIA: Oh, Friedrich is bound to be back by then. Joey isn't coming for a fortnight.

MRS VON AIGNER: You must miss him very much.

GENIA: As you can imagine, Mrs von Aigner. You know what it means to see so little of your son.

MRS VON AIGNER: I do indeed.

GENIA: Your son will be leaving you now for . . . years?

MRS VON AIGNER: Yes.

GENIA: In the South Sea Islands, he was telling me. I wonder whether you are not more fortunate than I am, Mrs von Aigner. You have your career, and you are such a celebrity. It must be so fulfilling.

MRS VON AIGNER: Yes, one would think so.

GENIA: Isn't it? For a woman to be only a mother . . . it isn't right, it seems to me sometimes. If that had been your only role in life, just Otto's mother, you'd never have allowed him to join the navy.

MRS VON AIGNER: And if I hadn't allowed it?

GENIA: Then he would have stayed at home with you.

MRS VON AIGNER: I have the impression, my dear, that I'd be

lucky to see more of him at home than when he's on the
high seas. What do you think?

GENIA: Oh. . . !

MRS VON AIGNER: In fact, Mrs Hofreiter, the sooner we free
ourselves of the illusion that we can ever possess our
children, the better. Particularly sons! They have us, but
we don't have them, even when they are under the same
roof. While they are small, they would sell us for a toy.
Later on . . . for even less.

GENIA: (*Shaking her head*) That is just . . . no, that . . . Can I
tell you something, Mrs von Aigner?

MRS VON AIGNER: (*Smiling*) Why not? It's just idle chatter.

GENIA: Actually, I'm just asking myself, when you made that
very – forgive me – melodramatic remark about people in
general – whether that doesn't have something to do with
the roles you have to play, so that life and melodrama
sometimes seem a little difficult to separate.

MRS VON AIGNER: (*Smiling*) Melodrama – do you think so?

GENIA: Because I have obviously got a lighter view of life than
you have, Mrs von Aigner. Your son seems to me to be
especially tender in his – I'm sure he thinks the world of
you. And if he ever were to 'sell' you, as you say, it
certainly wouldn't be over anything unworthy.

MRS VON AIGNER: (*After a short pause*) He's a man. One has to
look to the future . . . even sons, they all turn into men,
don't they?

(FRIEDRICH *appears on the balcony*.)

I would have thought you had some idea of what I mean.

FRIEDRICH: A familiar voice floats up to me and – yes, I
thought as much . . . How are you, Mrs von Aigner?

MRS VON AIGNER: Good evening, Mr Hofreiter.

GENIA: Do you need anything, Friedrich?

FRIEDRICH: Oh, no thank you. I've almost finished. I'll be right
down. I'm going away, you see.

MRS VON AIGNER: Yes, Mrs Hofreiter was telling me.

FRIEDRICH: See you in a minute then.

(*He leaves the balcony. Pause.*)

GENIA: Mrs von Aigner, everything you say seems so right, so unanswerable, but aren't you being just a little unfair?

MRS VON AIGNER: Perhaps so, Mrs Hofreiter . . . But after all, being unfair is our revenge.

(GENIA *looks at her in surprise.*)

Our only way of getting even for the wrongs done to us. Oh, I know what you're thinking – what does she want, this old actress? – Her marriage broke up aeons ago, and ever since, so they say, she's lived her life simply to please herself . . . She doesn't seem to have shed any tears for her husband . . . so what does she want? Isn't that what you think, Mrs Hofreiter?

GENIA: (*Somewhat embarrassed*) No one would deny that you had the right to live as you pleased . . .

MRS VON AIGNER: Quite so. And I'm not trying to say I feel anything like pain any more about those events which took place so long ago . . . or resentment either! But – I don't forget . . . that's all. Think of all the other things which I've forgotten since then! Happy things and sad things . . . all forgotten – as if they had never been! But not that. That remains as sharp and as complete as it was on that first day – not to be denied – that's what I'm trying to say, Mrs Hofreiter . . .

(OTTO *comes from the tennis court.*)

Good evening, Otto . . .

OTTO: Mother! Good evening.

MRS VON AIGNER: My darling! (*To* GENIA) Permit me . . . I've come to see you play.

(MRS VON AIGNER *and* OTTO *go to the tennis court.* GENIA *moves quickly to the house, but meets* FRIEDRICH *in the doorway. He is dressed in a grey travelling suit.*)

GENIA: Why – why – are you going away? (*Pause.*) You're not answerable to me, indeed you're not. But I really can't see why you should want to avoid the question.

FRIEDRICH: I need a change of air, a change of surroundings. In any event, I must get away from here.

GENIA: From here? . . . From me!

FRIEDRICH: Very well, from you!

GENIA: But why? What have I done to you?

FRIEDRICH: Nothing . . . who said you'd done anything to
me?

GENIA: You must explain, Friedrich . . . I'm completely . . . I
was prepared for anything except that . . . you should . . .
so suddenly . . . from one minute to the next – I mean
. . . I've been expecting us . . . to discuss things . . .

FRIEDRICH: I think it's not yet time to . . . talk . . . I've still
got to get myself clear about all kinds of things.

GENIA: Clear – ? What can be unclear? Listen . . . you had his
letter in your hand! You've read it, haven't you? If you
had doubted me before . . . which I simply don't believe
. . . since that evening, for God's sake, Friedrich, since
that evening you had his letter in your hand, you must
have had some idea – Friedrich, some idea what you mean
– what I feel – God – do I really have to tell you?

FRIEDRICH: No, of course not . . . That's just it. That
evening. Yes. Ever since then I've felt – forgive me, of
course you didn't mean to – but I felt that you were
somehow playing off Korsakow's suicide against me . . .
without knowing it, of course . . . And that – that makes
me just . . . a little upset . . .

GENIA: Friedrich! Have you gone. . . ?

FRIEDRICH: Without knowing it. I know you didn't see it like
that – Absolutely. I'm not saying you took any pride in
the fact that for your sake he . . . that you, so to speak,
drove him to kill himself . . . by rejecting him when he –
yes, I know all that . . .

GENIA: Well, if you know it –

FRIEDRICH: Yes, but the fact that it did happen at all – just
think about it . . . just think that poor Korsakow is now
rotting underground and you were the cause of it! The
innocent cause, and innocent in both senses, as I said.
Another man might go on his knees before you for that

93

very innocence, worship you . . . but I am not like that . . . no, it has distanced me from you.

GENIA: Friedrich!! . . .

FRIEDRICH: I would have understood it if you had been repelled by him. But you were not. On the contrary he attracted you . . . One might even say you were a little in love with him. Or if I had deserved your fidelity, if you had felt honour-bound to be faithful, as they call it, to a faithful husband – but I did not have that right . . . So the question I keep asking myself over and over again is: what did he die for?

GENIA: Friedrich!

FRIEDRICH: And, you see, the thought that your virtue . . . that something so abstract – at least compared to the terrible and irreversible fact of death – that your virtuousness drove a marvellous man to his grave, that to me is ghastly. Yes . . . I can't put it any other way . . . it'll pass, of course, this feeling . . . in time . . . in the mountains . . . and if we are apart for a few weeks . . . but at the moment, it is there – and I can't do anything about it . . . Yes, Genia, there you have me – Other men would feel differently, perhaps . . .
(GENIA *is silent.*)
I hope you won't take it badly that I – since you asked me – have brought it into the open. So much so, indeed, it hardly seems true again . . .

GENIA: It's true all right, Friedrich . . .
(*The others are approaching, from the court.*)

PAUL: Don't even ask me how I got on – tomorrow it's back to coaching for me.

MAUER: I'm sorry, Friedrich, but it's high time . . . Perhaps you could come on a later train . . .

FRIEDRICH: I'm all ready . . . (*Calling up*) Come on, Kathi – be quick! My overcoat and my small tan bag, on the divan in my dressing room.

MRS WAHL: Safe journey then, and all being well we'll see each other again.

ERNA: At Lake Vols.

MRS WAHL: I'll tell you what would be fun, Mrs Hofreiter – if you came too.

ERNA: Oh yes, Frau Genia.

GENIA: That's not possible, unfortunately – what with Joey coming . . .

FRIEDRICH: He's not coming all that soon. (*To* MAUER) When will we get to Lake Vols?

MAUER: In eight or ten days, I should think.

FRIEDRICH: Yes, Genia, that's an idea. Do think it over –

GENIA: All right, I'll . . . think it over.

(KATHI *comes out with the overcoat and the small bag.*)

MAUER: Goodbye then, Mrs Hofreiter.

(*He takes his leave of the others.*)

FRIEDRICH: Farewell, dear friends. What are you all going to do with yourselves today?

PAUL: This might be an idea – a moonlight trip to Holy Cross!

ERNA: I'm game.

MRS WAHL: On foot?

FRIEDRICH: That's not necessary. I'll send you the car back from the station.

PAUL: Three cheers for our noble benefactor!

FRIEDRICH: No demonstrations, I beg you. Adieu then. Enjoy yourselves, everybody. Goodbye, Genia. Come along, Mauer, we haven't got all day.

(FRIEDRICH *takes* GENIA's *hand, which she then lets fall limply.* FRIEDRICH *and* MAUER *leave through the house.* GENIA *stands still.* PAUL, ERNA *and* MRS WAHL *are standing together.* OTTO *and* MRS VON AIGNER *catch each other's eye.*)

OTTO: (*Taking leave of* GENIA) Ma'am, we must also . . .

GENIA: (*Quickly, pulling herself together*) You're going? And you, Mrs von Aigner? There's plenty of room in the car for everyone.

ERNA: Of course. Mr Kreindl can sit in front with the driver.

PAUL: Only too delighted.

OTTO: I feel I ought to point out that this moonlight drive will have to transcend the absence of a moon.

ERNA: We'll manage with the stars, Lieutenant.

MRS VON AIGNER: (*Looking at the sky*) I'm afraid you'll have to do without those, too.

ERNA: Then we'll take a leap into the dark.

GENIA: Yes, Erna, that might be the most exciting thing of all. (GENIA *starts to laugh. They all move off.*)

ACT THREE

The lobby of the Lake Vols Hotel. The entrance is a glass revolving door. There is a lift, stairs, a view of mountains, forests, etc. A curtain hangs over the entrance to the corridor leading to the dining room. By the entrance is the reception desk, behind which are the pigeon-holes for letters and keys, etc. Hotel lobby furniture. There is a certain amount of movement in the lobby, which, without interrupting the action, continues through the act at appropriate moments. Hikers and summer visitors come in from outside, guests go up in the lift, others use the stairs, occasionally a waiter. People read the papers or chat. A BELLBOY *by the lift. Behind the reception desk stands the porter,* ROSENSTOCK, *a ruddy, quite young man with a small black moustache, black hair, sly, good-natured eyes, friendly and shrewd. He hands newspapers to a* BELLBOY *who runs up the stairs with them and disappears. Two men in alpine clothes come in from outside and go straight into the dining room.* ROSENSTOCK *makes notes in a book. Two young* HIKERS *enter from outside, with rucksacks, climbing jackets, sticks, etc.*

FIRST HIKER: (*Full of beans*) Morning, all! – No, I'm a liar – good evening.

ROSENSTOCK: Your humble servant.

SECOND HIKER: Tell me, do you have two rooms with one bed?

FIRST HIKER: Or one room with two beds?

ROSENSTOCK: What is the gentleman's name?

SECOND HIKER: So, one has to introduce oneself here.

FIRST HIKER: Bogenheimer, student at law, from Halle. Born at Merseburg, of Protestant stock, and this . . .

SECOND HIKER: Archduke Ferdinand, travelling incognito.

ROSENSTOCK: (*Smiling slightly*) I only wished to inquire whether the gentlemen had booked rooms.

SECOND HIKER: Nay, lad, that we 'aven't.

ROSENSTOCK: (*Very politely*) Then I'm very sorry, but unfortunately we have nothing at all available.

FIRST HIKER: Not even a straw mattress to cling to?

ROSENSTOCK: Not even a palliasse.

FIRST HIKER: We've been on the hoof for fourteen hours.

ROSENSTOCK: That's a long time.

SECOND HIKER: I'm not moving.

FIRST HIKER: Did you hear that, Cerberus? My friend isn't moving.

ROSENSTOCK: *Bitte*. In our hall there's room for all.

FIRST HIKER: Ah, you're a poet, then?

ROSENSTOCK: Only in a crisis.

FIRST HIKER: What are we going to do then?

ROSENSTOCK: If the gentlemen would perhaps like to try the Alpenrose . . .

FIRST HIKER: Is that a hotel too?

ROSENSTOCK: In a manner of speaking.

FIRST HIKER: Do you think they'll have something there?

ROSENSTOCK: They always have something there.

FIRST HIKER: Very well. We'll take a sniff at the old Alpenrose. Up you get, old son.

SECOND HIKER: I'm not moving. If you get a room send a sedan chair.

FIRST HIKER: Kindly see that my friend is not disturbed. (*As he goes, singing the Schubert song . . .*) 'Das Wandern ist der Müllers Lust . . .'
(SECOND HIKER *makes himself comfortable and soon falls asleep. As* FIRST HIKER *exits . . .* PAUL KREINDL *arrives, in an elegant travelling suit, large top coat, green alpine hat with a chamois tuft, tan gloves, tennis racket and bag in his hand. A* BELLBOY *follows him with his luggage.*)

PAUL: Good day.

ROSENSTOCK: Your servant, Mr von Kreindl.

PAUL: Ah, who's this! You, my dear old Rosenstock! Are you here now? How will the Alpenrose get on without you?

ROSENSTOCK: I'm going up in the world, Mr von Kreindl.

From a thousand metres to fourteen hundred . . .

PAUL: You received my telegram?

ROSENSTOCK: Of course. Yes . . . You'll find numerous acquaintances here, Mr von Kreindl, sir. Mr von Hofreiter is here . . .

PAUL: Know him . . .

ROSENSTOCK: Mrs von Wahl with her son and daughter . . .

PAUL: Know them . . .

ROSENSTOCK: Dr Mauer . . .

PAUL: Know him . . .

ROSENSTOCK: Then there's Rhon the poet, who's here resting on his laurels.

PAUL: Ah, him too.

ROSENSTOCK: We had to put you on the fourth floor, I'm afraid.

PAUL: The sixth will do me. (*To the* BELLBOY) Take that stuff up. (*Retrieving his tennis racket*) Ah no, I'll hang on to that.

ROSENSTOCK: Mr Hofreiter has been on a climb since yesterday.

PAUL: One of the big ones?

ROSENSTOCK: Oh no. They were only going as far as the Hofbrand Hut. There were ladies with them. Mrs Rhon and Miss von Wahl.

PAUL: My dear Rosenstock, don't tell anyone I'm here. I'm going to give them a surprise!

(MRS WAHL *comes down the stairs in a summer dress which is a little too young for her.*)

MRS WAHL: (*Casually*) Oh, hello Paul. (*To* ROSENSTOCK) Are they still not back?

ROSENSTOCK: Not yet, madam.

PAUL: (*Disappointed*) How do you do, ma'am.

MRS WAHL: (*To* PAUL) I'm distraught. Erna has been out climbing since yesterday. She should have been back for lunch, now it's five o'clock. I've just been to her room – she's living as close as you can get to heaven already . . . her all over! – and she isn't back yet. I'm beside myself.

PAUL: It's quite a large party, I gather.

MRS WAHL: Gustl's there, of course, and Friedrich Hofreiter, and Dr Mauer and Mrs Rhon.

PAUL: Well, then, nothing can have happened. By the way, please, ma'am, don't tell anyone I'm here, if they happen to return while I'm changing.

MRS WAHL: Why?

PAUL: I'd like to surprise them, you see. (*Regretfully*) In your case, I'm afraid I didn't succeed.

MRS WAHL: You really have to forgive me that today, dear Paul, with all this worry.

PAUL: Well, perhaps some other time. Goodbye for now, ma'am, and don't say anything.
(*He goes up in the lift.*)

ROSENSTOCK: (*To* MRS WAHL) Madam really need not be concerned. After all, the party took a guide with them.

MRS WAHL: A guide just to go to the Hofbrand Hut? I say, I don't like the sound of that.

ROSENSTOCK: Only to carry the haversacks. And besides, your daughter is an excellent climber . . .

MRS WAHL: So was Dr Bernhaupt. And look what happened to him.

ROSENSTOCK: Yes . . . In the midst of life we are in death . . .

MRS WAHL: Look – would you please mind! . . .

ROSENSTOCK: Oh, sorry . . . I need hardly say that that does not apply to your daughter.

MRS WAHL: Rosenstock, I left a book with you, can I have it, by Rhon . . . with a yellow cover . . . Yes, that's the one . . . I'll sit here and read for a bit, if I can.

ROSENSTOCK: Ah, that's a book which will take your mind off anything, madam. He's a clever writer, Mr Rhon.
(MRS WAHL *sits down at one of the tables.* SERKNITZ *comes down the stairs, wearing woollen clothes and a hiking shirt.*)

SERKNITZ: (*To* ROSENSTOCK) Letters here yet?

ROSENSTOCK: Not yet, Mr von Serknitz. In about half an hour.

SERKNITZ: What a shambles!! The postman left ages ago.

ROSENSTOCK: But it has to be sorted, Mr von Serknitz.

SERKNITZ: Sorted!! You sit me down there, and I'll sort the whole lot for you in a quarter of an hour. Typical Austrian slovenliness. And then you complain about the poor tourist trade.

ROSENSTOCK: We're not complaining, Mr von Serknitz. We're overflowing.

SERKNITZ: The Austrians don't deserve the place.

ROSENSTOCK: But we've got it, Mr von Serknitz.

SERKNITZ: You may dispense with the von, Porter. I'm not impressed by that ploy. In fact it's not the post I've come about -- I've come about the laundry.

ROSENSTOCK: Please, Mr Serknitz, I have nothing to do with . . .

SERKNITZ: Nor anybody else. The maid upstairs tells me to go to the desk. I've been waiting for my laundry for three days.

ROSENSTOCK: I'm really very sorry. However, here comes the manager.

SERKNITZ: Not alone – as usual.

(DR VON AIGNER *has just arrived from outside with a very beautiful Spanish girl. He takes leave of her and she goes up in the lift.* DR VON AIGNER *is a man of over fifty, still very good-looking. Elegant alpine knickerbocker suit; black hair flecked with grey, twisted moustache, monocle; amiable but a little affected.*)

Ah, Manager . . .

DR VON AIGNER: (*Barely polite*) Be with you in a moment . . . (*To* ROSENSTOCK) My dear Rosenstock, His Excellency Wondra is arriving tomorrow instead of Thursday, and requires, as you know, four rooms.

ROSENSTOCK: Four rooms, sir, for tomorrow . . . How am I supposed to do that? That means people will have to . . . pardon me, sir, but that means I'll have to kill people.

DR VON AIGNER: Fine, Rosenstock, just be discreet about it. (*To* SERKNITZ, *introducing himself*) Dr von Aigner . . . How can I be of service to you?

SERKNITZ: (*With some embarrassment, which he seeks to conceal by his assured manner*) Serknitz . . . I was just . . . I must express my irritation, or at least my dismay . . . To put it bluntly, the way this hotel is run is a disgrace.

DR VON AIGNER: I'm dumbstruck. What is your complaint, Mr Serknitz?

SERKNITZ: I can't get my laundry back, you see. I've been asking for it for three days. It puts me in an awful spot.

DR VON AIGNER: Yes, I see. But why don't you ask the chambermaid . . .

SERKNITZ: You're the manager! My principle is always to go to the top. Really, I get very little pleasure in appearing in this get-up among your countesses and dollar princesses.

DR VON AIGNER: Forgive me, Mr Serknitz, but we have no rules here about how one must dress.

SERKNITZ: No rules!! . . . Do you really think it isn't noticeable how different people are treated here?

DR VON AIGNER: My dear sir – !

SERKNITZ: I will tell you to your face, my dear sir! – if the King of England, or His Excellency Wondra stood here instead of plain Carl-Maria von Serknitz you would adopt a very different tone. Yes indeed. You would be well advised to put a notice over the entrance: 'Some hope, all ye who enter here, unless you're a baron, a bank director, or an American.'

DR VON AIGNER: That would not correspond to the true state of affairs, Mr Serknitz.

SERKNITZ: Just because I didn't arrive here by limousine I haven't the right to the same consideration as any trust magnate or minister of state? – is that your attitude? The man hasn't been born who can get away with treating me in that high-handed fashion . . . Whether he wears a monocle or not.

DR VON AIGNER: (*As calm as ever*) If anything about my manner is a personal affront to you, Mr Serknitz, I am of course at your disposal.

SERKNITZ: Ha ha! So now it's swords or pistols, is it! That's a
good one. You must take out a patent on that – one complains
that some shirts haven't been delivered, and they shoot you
dead to boot. Listen, Herr Direktor, if you think that sort of
thing is going to be particularly good for business, you are
labouring under a massive delusion. I would leave this joke
hotel, this Eldorado of snobs, swindlers and stockbroker
Jews, on the spot, by special express, but for the fact that I
don't intend to make you a present of my laundry. For the
moment, I will go and see if it has been returned. In the
meantime, your humble servant, sir.
(*He leaves up the stairs.*)

DR VON AIGNER: Good day, Mr Serknitz. (*To* MRS WAHL, *to
whom he has already nodded during the conversation*) Good
afternoon, madam.

MRS WAHL: I wish I had your self-control.

DR VON AIGNER: Why? What's the matter?

MRS WAHL: I'm in a terrible state. Our party isn't back yet.

DR VON AIGNER: Oh, but I beg you, madam . . . No one has
ever failed to come back from the Hofbrand Hut. It's only a
stroll . . . (*Sitting down next to her*) May I?

MRS WAHL: *May* you? One must be grateful if for once you aren't
frantically – or romantically – busy.

DR VON AIGNER: Frantically . . . romantically. . . ? That
doesn't sound like you – a nice lady like you couldn't be that
wicked.

MRS WAHL: No . . . it's Rhon.

DR VON AIGNER: Yes, I thought so . . . he's a poet, Mr Rhon,
yes. What a lovely brooch you have there.

MRS WAHL: Yes, it's quite pretty, isn't it?

DR VON AIGNER: Peasant baroque.

MRS WAHL: And not at all dear.

DR VON AIGNER: Quite delightful.

MRS WAHL: Not that it was exactly cheap. Swaten in Salzburg
always puts these things by for me. He really knows my
taste.

(ALBERTUS RHON *comes downstairs.*)

RHON: Good day, madam. Good evening, Herr Direktor. Well, aren't our mountaineers back yet?

MRS WAHL: They are not!

RHON: They'll be here soon . . . Perhaps they've breakfasted too well . . . My wife, anyway.

(*A very pretty* ITALIAN GIRL *comes up to* DR VON AIGNER, *speaks with an Italian accent.*)

GIRL: Signor . . . Herr Direktor . . . one can speak with you?

DR VON AIGNER: *Prego* . . . Signorina . . .

(*He goes upstage with her.*)

RHON: (*To* MRS WAHL) His latest conquest.

MRS WAHL: What, her? You pointed out a different one yesterday.

RHON: It was a different one yesterday. Oh yes, what a man! You have no idea of the swathe he has cut through the district. Haven't you been struck, for instance, by the similarity between Aigner and the head waiter?

MRS WAHL: You think the head waiter is his son?

RHON: His nephew anyway. Yes, the way he gets about, even his nephews look like him.

MRS WAHL: How can you be in any sort of mood to make jokes! They should have been back for lunch. It's half-past five now. I blame myself for not going with them.

RHON: You're quite wrong to do so. It would only have made rescue more difficult, and added to the casualty list.

MRS WAHL: I find your jokes in horribly bad taste.

RHON: Well, I'm writing a tragedy.

(DR VON AIGNER *has come forward again.*)

Still, they ought to be back by now. My wife at least. I'm accustomed to being received by her when I re-enter the real world *entre actes*. We like to spend the interval together.

DR VON AIGNER: Usually at the buffet.

RHON: (*Clapping him on the shoulder good-humouredly*) True, true. Tell me, anyway, is it really such a straightforward business, this Hofbrand Hut.

DR VON AIGNER: As I told you, a stroll. Even I could manage the Hofbrand Hut.

MRS WAHL: Why didn't you go with them, Dr von Aigner? I wouldn't have worried then.

DR VON AIGNER: Yes . . . unfortunately I have my hands full here, as you were remarking, dear lady. Furthermore, since the Hofbrand Hut is about as far as I can go I'd rather not go at all.

RHON: Very good. But another thought has just occurred to me, Herr Direktor – doesn't the climb to your peak start from the Hut? To the Aignerturm, I mean?

DR VON AIGNER: Yes, it was mine once! No longer. But no one else's either.

RHON: It must be an extraordinary feeling, to sit at the foot of a peak one was the first to go up and find oneself no longer able even to . . . yes, one might venture a simile here . . .
(MRS WAHL *gives a little scream*.)
No, I see what you mean.

MRS WAHL: So what it comes down to, they're all up the Aignerturm.

RHON: (*Also somewhat alarmed*) Why do you think that?

MRS WAHL: Of course they are. Otherwise they'd be back by now. They've got a guide with them, too. Dr von Aigner, you're all in it together –

DR VON AIGNER: I promise you . . .

RHON: Isn't that a guide?

MRS WAHL: Where?
(*The guide* PENN *is standing by the* PORTER. RHON *and* MRS WAHL *rush over to him*.)
Penn! Were you with the Hofreiter party?

PENN: Aye.
(*The next five lines overlap*.)

MRS WAHL: Where's my daughter?

RHON: Where's my wife?

MRS WAHL: Say something.

RHON: When did they get back?

MRS WAHL: Where are the others? Why are you alone? What's happened?

PENN: (*Smiling*) They're all back here with me, Mrs. The young lady managed splendidly.

MRS WAHL: What do you mean?

RHON: Where were you, then?

PENN: We've been up the Aignerturm.

MRS WAHL: (*With a quiet shriek*) Oh my God!

RHON: My wife up the Aignerturm? It's not possible.

PENN: No, the little fat one didn't go up. Just Miss Erna, Hofreiter and Dr Mauer.

RHON: And what about my wife?

MRS WAHL: And my son?

PENN: They waited for us in the hut, till we got back.

MRS WAHL: So where are they, then?

PENN: The ladies and gentlemen came in by the tap room, so's not to cause a flap.

MRS WAHL: I must go upstairs, I must see Erna. (*To* DR VON AIGNER) Oh, you . . .

(*She goes to the lift; because the lift is upstairs she rings in despair. To* AIGNER) Why does your lift spend all its time at the fourth floor? That's another funny thing about this hotel. (*To* RHON) Aren't you coming up?

RHON: I can wait.

(*The lift comes down with the* BELLBOY. RHON *draws* MRS WAHL *aside.*)

Psst! Just look at that lift boy.

MRS WAHL: Why?

RHON: Amazing similarity.

(MRS WAHL *enters the lift.* GUSTL WAHL *arrives, in an elegant summer suit, speaking with a kind of affected drawl, at times with a calculated air of significance. He's always good-humoured.*)

GUSTL: Good evening, Mr Rhon. (*To* DR VON AIGNER) How do you do, Mr Aignerturm.

RHON: Gustl!

DR VON AIGNER: (*To* PENN) So, you got to the top?

PENN: Yes, Mr Aigner. It wasn't easy.

DR VON AIGNER: I can imagine.

PENN: We had to duck sharpish a few times. And as for the last hundred feet, God knows . . .

DR VON AIGNER: But up top was good.

PENN: Mr Aigner knows right enough. It's always good up top, especially on the Aignerturm.

GUSTL: (*To* RHON) Must congratulate you on your wife. Plays an excellent game of dominoes.

RHON: You played dominoes the whole time? While the others were suspended between life and death? I'm not surprised about my wife. Women have no imagination. But you should know better.

GUSTL: We didn't play dominoes all the time. At first I tried to engage your wife in conversation.

RHON: About Buddhist philosophy, I presume.

GUSTL: Mainly.

RHON: My wife isn't interested in Buddha.

GUSTL: Yes, I got that impression too. That's why I suggested dominoes.

DR VON AIGNER: Since when have they had a domino set up there?

GUSTL: One can always find a domino set. On this occasion one found it in one's rucksack. I never take a step without a set of dominoes. I've spent years in the study of the game.
(MRS RHON *arrives, a small, pretty, rather plump woman. She throws her arms round her husband's neck.*)

MRS RHON: Here I am again!

RHON: Come, come, that'll do. We're not alone . . .

DR VON AIGNER: Please don't mind us.

RHON: (*Coolly*) Well, did you enjoy it?

MRS RHON: It was glorious.

RHON: I hear you played dominoes.

MRS RHON: Are you cross with me? I won.

RHON: Well, it's better than trying to climb the scenery anyway.

MRS RHON: Do you know, I really was tempted for a moment. Only, they didn't want to take me.

RHON: Now listen, don't start getting ideas like that. I'm not going to have the pleasure of my solitude ruined by having to worry about you. When you're not with me, I don't want to have to think about you at all.

GUSTL: That's why she doesn't think about you either, Rhon old man. Take my word for it, you're going to get an awful shock one day. It was sheer luck that I wasn't your wife's type.

RHON: Tell me, Gustl, why are you so tactless?

GUSTL: I do it to impress. And anyway – what is tact! A third-rate virtue. Even the word is quite new. You won't find it in Latin, nor Greek, nor – most significantly – in Sanskrit.

MRS RHON: (*To* RHON) Well then, what have you been doing in the meanwhile? Did you get any further?

RHON: End of Act Three, the audience rushes deeply moved into the bar.

MRS RHON: Then I've come back at the right moment.

RHON: Yes, only this time it's a short interval. First thing tomorrow I'm locking myself away again so that I don't have my mood disrupted by having to look at all those stupid faces at lunch. And you'll be free to play dominoes.

GUSTL: Madam, get a divorce. How can anyone marry a poet? They're a subspecies. It was much better in the olden days, when one kept a poet like a slave or a barber – a tradition, incidentally, which survives in Isfahan – but to let a poet run around loose is plain silly.

FRIEDRICH: (*Entering in an elegant hiking suit*) Good evening, ladies and gentlemen, how's the lovely poet's wife? What, you've changed already? You've been quick.

DR VON AIGNER: (*Who is now standing near* ROSENSTOCK) Hallo there, Hofreiter.

FRIEDRICH: Good evening, Aigner. (*To* ROSENSTOCK) Nothing for me? Telegram? Letter? That's odd. (*To* VON AIGNER) Well, I can tell you that nothing has changed in the least up

there, not on top anyway. Of course, the route has got more
difficult. If it keeps on crumbling, it'll be certain suicide.

DR VON AIGNER: Yes, Penn told me.

FRIEDRICH: You know when you come to that gully, three
hundred metres below the summit . . .

DR VON AIGNER: (*Interrupting him*) I'd rather not hear about it.
How did the little lady get on?

FRIEDRICH: Erna? Simply splendidly.

DR VON AIGNER: Taking her with you . . . I must say . . .

FRIEDRICH: She took *us*. I hadn't the slightest intention of
climbing that mountain again. Where's Mauer, by the way?

DR VON AIGNER: I haven't seen him yet.

RHON: Tell me, Hofreiter, how did you actually feel when you
passed that place . . .

FRIEDRICH: What place? . . . My God, seven years is a long
time. I've forgotten most things that lie much closer in the
past.

RHON: Well, yes . . . I suppose one often passes by a place
where someone fell down, and fails to recognize it. Don't
you think. . . ?

FRIEDRICH: If only you knew how little I feel in the mood for
philosophizing, Mr Rhon . . .

PAUL: (*Coming rapidly down the stairs*) Your humble servant, Mr
Hofreiter!

FRIEDRICH: (*Rather offhand*) Ah – hello there, Paulie.

PAUL: Good evening, Mr Rhon. I've had the pleasure once
before . . . Well, first of all, I've got loads of greetings for
you. First from your good lady, then from Captain
Stanzides, the Natters, from Mrs von Aigner, and from
young Mr von Aigner . . .

FRIEDRICH: Allow me to introduce you . . . Mr Paul Kreindl
– the manager, Dr von Aigner.

PAUL: Ah . . . most pleased . . . (*He stops, disconcerted; then,
collecting himself, to* DR VON AIGNER) Actually I have the
pleasure of knowing your son.

DR VON AIGNER: Unfortunately, I haven't.

FRIEDRICH: So what's new in Baden? (*Quietly*) Do you know – if perhaps my wife is coming?

PAUL: Your wife, coming here? Sorry, she said nothing to me.

FRIEDRICH: Are they amusing themselves all right?

PAUL: Wonderfully! Just the other day we were all together at the Arena Theatre. No doubt your good lady has written you all about it.

FRIEDRICH: Yes, of course.

PAUL: And before that a travelling fair set up in the field by the house. We joined in with the people. We danced.

FRIEDRICH: My wife too?

PAUL: Yes, absolutely – with the Lieutenant . . . By the way, at the Arena we caused a great sensation when the actors suddenly spotted the famous Mrs von Aigner in our box. After that they more or less played to us, actually.

RHON: What was the play?

PAUL: I never noticed. Lot of Frenchmen in wigs. I think it rhymed. Yes . . . people in wigs rhyming . . . The girl had consumption. Wasn't that your dear wife? Excuse me, gentlemen.

(*He exits.*)

RHON: One pours out one's life's blood for people like that.

(*He follows* PAUL. FRIEDRICH *remains with* DR VON AIGNER. FRIEDRICH *lights a cigarette and sits down.*)

DR VON AIGNER: I had no idea that my former family had the run of your house.

FRIEDRICH: Yes, one sees them from time to time. In particular, your wife – as was – has become great friends with mine. And I sometimes play tennis with Otto. He plays very well. In fact he does you credit altogether. Perhaps he's a future admiral of the fleet.

DR VON AIGNER: You're telling me about a young man who's a stranger to me.

FRIEDRICH: Tell me, Aigner, have you really no desire to see him again?

DR VON AIGNER: Again? The most you could say is, be

introduced to him. That naval officer has nothing to do with the boy I saw twenty years ago when I kissed him for the last time. (*Pause.*) Actually, it is an extraordinary coincidence.

FRIEDRICH: What is?

DR VON AIGNER: That you should start talking to me about my son . . . Just after you've come back from up there . . . Do you know when I took on that climb? It was just after I . . . separated from my wife.

FRIEDRICH: Do you mean there was a connection?

DR VON AIGNER: In a way . . . I'm not quite claiming that I was flirting with death – there are simpler deaths available – but at that time life didn't mean very much to me. And perhaps I wanted to provoke a kind of divine retribution.

FRIEDRICH: Listen, if every erring husband started climbing up the nearest cliff . . . the Dolomites would afford a very quaint spectacle. Anyway, you didn't do anything worse than a lot of others.

DR VON AIGNER: The measure is in the effect on the other person. My wife loved me very much.

FRIEDRICH: All the more reason for her not to be so unforgiving.

DR VON AIGNER: Possibly. But I loved her very much too. That's the trouble! I loved her inexpressibly . . . like no other woman, before or since . . . It was because I loved her so much – and was still capable of deceiving her – that's what made it irreparable. You see, my dear Hofreiter, that left her utterly confused, about me and about the whole world. After that there was absolutely nothing on earth she could count on . . . no possibility of trust, that's what drove her away from me. And I could understand that. I should even have been able to foresee it.

FRIEDRICH: Well, that being the case, I have to ask why . . .

DR VON AIGNER: Why I betrayed her? *You* ask *me*? Haven't you ever thought what a strange uncharted country is human behaviour? So many contradictions find room in us – love and deceit . . . loyalty and betrayal . . . worshipping one woman, yet longing for another, or several others. We try to bring order into our lives as best we can; but that very order has something unnatural about it. The natural condition is chaos. Yes, Hofreiter, the soul . . . is an undiscovered country as the poet once said . . . though it could equally well have been the manager of a hotel.

FRIEDRICH: The hotel manager wasn't so far wrong . . . yes. (*Pause.*) The pity of it is that your wife had to find out . . .

DR VON AIGNER: . . . I told her.

FRIEDRICH: What? – You told her? –

DR VON AIGNER: Yes. I had to. I worshipped her. I owed it to her and to myself. It would have been cowardice not to. One shouldn't try to have things so easy. Don't you agree. . . ?

FRIEDRICH: Shows great nobility – or affectation. Or tactics . . . or convenience . . .

DR VON AIGNER: Or all three, which would also have been possible. Because the soul . . . and so forth.

MRS WAHL: (*Coming down from upstairs*) Ah, there he is!

FRIEDRICH: How are you, Mrs Wahl?

MRS WAHL: I'm never going to say another word to you, Friedrich. What if she'd fallen? Could you ever have faced me again? And I've finished with Dr Mauer, too. Where is he then? It's quite monstrous.

FRIEDRICH: But, Mama Wahl, Erna would have climbed up with or without us.

MRS WAHL: You should have tied her up.

FRIEDRICH: But she was, Mama Wahl. We were all tied up together, on the one rope.

MRS WAHL: It should have been a strait-jacket.

ERNA: (*Entering in a white summer dress*) Good evening.

DR VON AIGNER: Greetings, Erna. How are you?
(*He takes both of her hands and kisses her on the forehead.*)
May I. . . ?

FRIEDRICH: Like the aged Liszt and the young lady pianist.

ERNA: More like quite a young lady pianist with a not yet particularly aged Liszt.

DR VON AIGNER: Nevertheless, Erna . . .

MRS WAHL: Yes – I should think so!

ERNA: It was the most wonderful experience I've ever had.

DR VON AIGNER: Ah yes – at the summit! Even so, I hope that
there are some even more wonderful experiences ahead of
you, Fraulein Erna.

ERNA: That would scarcely be possible. Oh – life might well
seem wonderful again, no doubt – but that death should
seem so completely unimportant – that's the true wonder,
and it could only happen at such a moment.

(*Meanwhile, the post has arrived.* ROSENSTOCK *sorts letters,*
GUESTS *arrive, take their correspondence, etc. And* PAUL
returns, followed by RHON, MRS WAHL, GUSTL.)

PAUL: Miss Erna, allow me to lay out my admiration at your
feet!

ERNA: Hello there, Paul, how are you?

PAUL: Oh God – damn it – sorry . . . isn't *anyone* surprised to
see me?

FRIEDRICH: (*Sitting down*) Look, Paul, it's much more
surprising that *we're* here.

(DR VON AIGNER *is standing to one side with a beautiful
French girl.*)

RHON: (*To* MRS WAHL) Look at that, ma'am, that's tomorrow's.
He's stocking up.

ERNA: (*To* MRS WAHL, *who has collected her letters from*
ROSENSTOCK) Well, Mama?

MRS WAHL: From home. (*To* FRIEDRICH) Ah, there's a card
from your wife. She sends her best wishes to you,
Friedrich.

FRIEDRICH: (*Rising*) Really? Ah, there's one for me, too.

MRS RHON: (*To* GUSTL, *who has laid his correspondence on his
forehead*) What are you doing?

GUSTL: I never read letters any more.

MRS WAHL: He simply presses them to his forehead and absorbs
the contents. (*To* FRIEDRICH) Well, is she coming after all?

FRIEDRICH: No.

RHON: (*Sitting and reading his letters*) Just listen to this. It's unbelievable. Queries from correspondents! At what age did you first experience the joys of physical love? Have you ever been aware of any perverted inclinations?

FRIEDRICH: And have you?

RHON: I should have been a businessman – they never get asked. Alas, I never had a head for business, so I became a poet.

FRIEDRICH: I often wonder if it's only because of their shortcomings that poets become poets.

RHON: What do you mean?

FRIEDRICH: I imagine that many poets are born criminals, only they lack the necessary courage; or libertines who shrink from the expense . . .

RHON: And do you know what manufacturers of incandescent light bulbs usually are, Mr Hofreiter? Incandescent-light-bulb manufacturers, that's all.

FRIEDRICH: If only that were true . . .

(*A* BELLBOY *brings* FRIEDRICH *a letter. He opens it, smiles and bites his lip.* ERNA *has noticed this.*)

MRS WAHL: Well, you must excuse me, I still have to change . . . come, illustrious poet . . . (*To* MRS RHON) with your muse . . .

MRS RHON: (*As* GUSTL *opens one of his letters*) But you're reading it.

GUSTL: I have to verify my gift . . . yes . . . yes . . . yes . . . I am amazing.

(MRS RHON *and* GUSTL *go upstage and leave.* DR VON AIGNER *goes to* ROSENSTOCK, *then leaves.* RHON *goes likewise. The lobby is almost empty.*)

ERNA: (*Looking over* FRIEDRICH's *shoulder*) Love letter?

FRIEDRICH: Guess who from? Mauer. He's just received an urgent telegram from Vienna. Had to leave immediately . . . he's gone . . . asks me to convey his respects . . .

ERNA: I thought it would be something like that.

FRIEDRICH: So did I . . . Yes, Erna, one really oughtn't to roll around on the grass fifty feet from a hut with twenty windows.

ERNA: You think he saw?

FRIEDRICH: Probably.

ERNA: And do you think it would have made any difference if he hadn't? We wouldn't even have had to look at each other for him to notice, just as the others noticed . . .

FRIEDRICH: What is there for them to notice?

ERNA: Our feelings for each other.

FRIEDRICH: But, Erna, how can these people . . . ?

ERNA: Perhaps we have a sort of lovers' glow around our heads, like a halo.

(FRIEDRICH *laughs*.)

Yes, it must be something like that – I've often thought so.

FRIEDRICH: It should have been me who left, Erna.

ERNA: Yes, that would have been much more sensible.

FRIEDRICH: You shouldn't be such a flirt.

ERNA: I really am not.

FRIEDRICH: Then what are you?

ERNA: I'm just the woman I am.

FRIEDRICH: There you have the advantage of me. I am not the man I was. I've gone mad since that kiss yesterday . . . Come closer, Erna. (*He takes her hand*.) Sit down here by me.

ERNA: Now don't get carried away.

FRIEDRICH: Erna, I didn't close my eyes last night.

ERNA: I'm sorry. I slept splendidly. I took my blanket out into the meadow – our meadow – and slept in the open . . . wrapped in your coat.

FRIEDRICH: Erna, Erna! I'm in a state to do something madly foolish. I suddenly understand all that nonsense I used to mock in other people . . . the faithful vigil under a lady's window . . . the serenading of one's mistress . . . (*With gestures*) I understand how one might duel with naked blades for love's favour, or throw oneself off a precipice for love unrequited.

ERNA: Unrequited?

FRIEDRICH: (*Seriously*) Don't deceive yourself, Erna. Yesterday evening . . . the whole thing, the moment up there on the summit, pressing each other's hands, the sense of belonging together, the overpowering feeling of joy, it was all just a kind of tipsiness – drunk on altitude. I mean for you. It all comes from being three thousand metres up in the sky, with the thin air, and the danger. It was very little to do with me personally.

ERNA: Why do you say that? I've loved you since I was seven. Not counting interruptions, of course. But recently I've got it very badly again. Seriously. And then yesterday and today – and up there – and now! Oh God, Friedrich, all I want to do is to get hold of your hair and run my fingers through it.

FRIEDRICH: Careful – that really isn't necessary. Listen, Erna – I want to ask you something.

ERNA: Then ask me.

FRIEDRICH: All right – what would you think if . . . listen – pay attention! – I'm quite sensible again. I want to get a divorce from Genia . . . and marry you, Erna.

(ERNA *laughs.*)

Why . . . are you laughing?

ERNA: Because you were only just saying that you were in a state to do something madly foolish.

FRIEDRICH: Perhaps it wouldn't be if we just took it for what it is. I know, Erna, you won't always love me.

ERNA: But you will always love me!!

FRIEDRICH: That is more probable. Anyway . . . as for eternity! What does it mean? Next year one climbs up another little peak, and that's the end of eternity! Or another beginning. All I know is this. I know with absolute certainty that I cannot exist without you. I'm faint with longing for you, I won't be able to think or work any more, or occupy myself with ordinary life until . . . until I hold you in my arms, Erna.

ERNA: Why didn't you come out and fetch your coat last night?

FRIEDRICH: I beg you, Erna, don't tease me. Look, just say no, and that's an end of it. They can still get Mauer back. I have no interest in making a public spectacle of myself.
(*A gong sounds. The* HIKER *who has gone to sleep at the beginning of the Act wakes up from a dream, gets up, screams, howls and crashes out across the full width of the stage.* MRS WAHL *comes down the stairs. Other* GUESTS *gather, moving to the dining room,* DR VON AIGNER *among them.*)
Heavens, the way we've chatted on . . . now I haven't got time to change.

MRS WAHL: You're handsome enough as you are. Where's Dr Mauer, by the way?

FRIEDRICH: Oh yes, that's right – he sends his respects, he had a telegram and had to leave at once.

MRS WAHL: A telegram – Dr Mauer? That's odd . . . someone's keeping something from me. He's fallen! He's dead!

FRIEDRICH: Now look, Mama Wahl, do you believe we could all be sitting around chatting if . . .

MRS WAHL: With you one can never tell.

FRIEDRICH: At the very least we'd be chatting in black gloves.
(SERKNITZ *enters in white tie and tails. He goes to* DR VON AIGNER.)

SERKNITZ: I have the honour, sir, to present myself, Herr von Aigner. Serknitz. My laundry has arrived, and I immediately took the liberty of attiring myself in the costume appropriate to the pretensions of your hotel.

DR VON AIGNER: Mr von Serknitz . . . You look absolutely ravishing.
(SERKNITZ *goes into the dining room.* MRS WAHL, DR VON AIGNER, MRS RHON, GUSTL, RHON *and others likewise go into the dining room.* ERNA *and* FRIEDRICH *are left.*)

FRIEDRICH: Do you want to be my wife?

ERNA: Wife? – No.

FRIEDRICH: Right, fine.

ERNA: Perhaps later on.

FRIEDRICH: Later – ?

ERNA: Go on reading your letters.

FRIEDRICH: What for? The whole factory can go up with an incandescent bang for all I care. Everything can go to hell. What does that mean – later! Life isn't long enough. I'm not giving you time to consider. A kiss like yesterday's is binding. It binds you to an immediate parting or to an unconditional surrender. I can't wait. I won't wait. Say no, and I leave today.

ERNA: I'm not teasing you. I know what our kiss bound me to.

FRIEDRICH: Erna, think about what you are saying. If your door is locked tonight, I'll smash it down and that'll be the end of us.

ERNA: It will not be the end of us.

FRIEDRICH: Erna. . . !

ERNA: Haven't you always known that I belong to you?

FRIEDRICH: Erna . . . Erna . . .

ERNA: I love you!

(*They enter the dining room.*)

ACT FOUR

The same scene as in Act Two. A summer afternoon.
In the garden sit MRS NATTER'S *two children, a nine-year-old* GIRL
and a seven-year-old BOY, *with their French* NANNY, *who is*
showing them pictures in a book. From the house drift GENIA,
NATTER, MRS WAHL, STANZIDES, GUSTL, PAUL, ERNA, OTTO
and ADELE NATTER.

GENIA: Do you like the pictures?

CHILDREN: Oh yes.

GENIA: You must ask your Mama to bring you back on Sunday
because Joey's bound to be here by then. Well, what would
you like to do now?

GUSTL: I'll show them a marvellous game that the good little
Hindu boys and girls play on the banks of the River
Ganges. Would you lend me your parasol, Mademoiselle?
Thank you very much. Watch carefully. So – I draw three
concentric circles on the ground . . .

NATTER: Well, I must say the welcome-home dinner for our
distinguished host was first rate. What a pity he couldn't be
here.

GENIA: He must have been held up at the factory.

NATTER: Small wonder after three weeks away.

GUSTL: One has a diameter of a metre . . .

MRS WAHL: Did you telephone the office, Genia?

GENIA: I didn't think it was necessary.

GUSTL: The middle one three-quarters of a metre . . .

GENIA: I was sure he'd be back by noon after yesterday's
telegram from Innsbruck.

GUSTL: Please! – The inside one half a metre. The Hindu
children hit it to a millimetre. Now watch carefully. You
draw one tangent along the outer circle.

ERNA: Let's go and play tennis.

PAUL: With the greatest of pleasure.

GUSTL: A second tangent at right angles to that one, along the middle circle.

PAUL: Ma'am? Lieutenant?

GUSTL: A third parallel to the first tangent along the inner circle.

ADELE: I won't play straight after a meal.

GUSTL: Thus you get segments, like so.

OTTO: I'm sure you'll permit me to finish my coffee.

GUSTL: Now in the outermost segment to the east . . .
(*He takes a small compass out of his pocket.*)

MRS WAHL: He always carries a compass.

GUSTL: Well, it's beyond me how anyone with a sense of propriety if not of direction could go around without one. So . . . East is there. In the outermost segment one places a baby tortoise . . .
(*He takes a tortoise from his pocket, and places it on the ground.*)
In the west segment a scorpion . . .
(*He brings his closed fist from his pocket. The children begin to cry.*)

ADELE: You just stop that, Gustl! Ma'm'selle – *s'il vous plaît* – Oh lord! (*She abandons French.*) Please, Nanny, would you take the children to play in the meadow. (*To the* CHILDREN) You'll be safe there from scorpions and tangents.
(NANNY *goes off with the* CHILDREN. STANZIDES *picks up a paper and starts reading.*)

STANZIDES: Listen to this! 'We have a report from the Lake Vols Hotel that a few days ago a young lady from Vienna, Miss Erna Wahl, accompanied by two Viennese climbers, the manufacturer Friedrich Hofreiter and the well-known physician Dr Mauer, climbed the Aignerturm, known as one of the most notoriously dangerous . . .'

ERNA: Come on, Paul.

PAUL: Yes – today we'll only play singles. A singles tournament; I hope Mr Hofreiter comes in time to take part. Today we must settle the positions once and for all. . . !

MRS WAHL: (*To* STANZIDES) How does it go on?

STANZIDES: (*Continues reading*) '. . . known as one of the most notoriously dangerous peaks in the south-western Dolomites. It was there that seven years ago Dr Bernhaupt . . .'

MRS WAHL: Yes, my dear Genia, those two dragged my Erna up mountains like that. I've never been so angry in my life as I was with Dr Mauer and your husband.

GUSTL: The two of them took one look at Mama and packed their bags.

GENIA: (*Looking at* ERNA, *smiling*) Yes, it seems that Friedrich's guilty conscience made him restless. I got a postcard from a different place every day – Caprile, Pordio and heaven knows where.

(PAUL *and* ERNA *leave for the tennis court.* MRS WAHL *has got hold of the newspaper and is leafing through it.*)

NATTER: You must be very proud, Mrs Wahl, now that Erna is a celebrity.

MRS WAHL: Proud? – me? What is this paper, actually?

GENIA: I don't know. I haven't seen it before. Who brought it?

MRS WAHL: There's an item underlined in red ink.

STANZIDES: I wouldn't pay any attention to anything underlined in red in a paper like that.

MRS WAHL: But this is extraordinary.

ADELE:
GUSTL: } What is?
GENIA:

MRS WAHL: (*Reading*) 'During the past few days a curious rumour has gathered force – and an accumulation of detail – in Viennese society. We pass it on with due discretion. It concerns the suicide of a world-famous pianist, who, at the beginning of the summer, was much in the limelight and then came under the shadow of what was not very satisfactorily explained by the hallowed phrase "a sudden brainstorm". According to the above-mentioned rumour the cause of the suicide was "an American duel"; with a difference. This was not, as is usual, a case of a black ball, but two white and one red . . .'

ADELE: Two white and one red . . . what does that mean?

STANZIDES: Billiards. And a black ball is obviously a bullet.

GENIA: (*Calmly, after a nervous pause*) But Friedrich lost that
billiard game with Korsakow. So it couldn't have been an
American duel . . . because in an American duel it's the
loser who has to shoot himself; so it would have been
Friedrich, wouldn't it?
(*Pause.*)

MRS WAHL: (*Understanding at last*) Ah, that billiard game. Your
husband sent the cigars round to Korsakow at the hotel the
next morning . . . That's right! I'd swear to that in court!

GUSTL: Mama, you won't be needed to swear. No one bothers
about this sort of thing.

STANZIDES: It is unbelievable that one is more or less helpless
against this sort of outrage. Especially as no names are
mentioned.

NATTER: They're too careful for that.
(STANZIDES *and* ADELE *move towards the tennis court, and
unhurriedly depart.*)

MRS WAHL: All the same . . . How does something like that get
into the papers? And why should Friedrich and
Korsakow . . .

GUSTL: Mama!

MRS WAHL: What a good idea. Yes. Let's go and watch the
tennis.
(MRS WAHL, GUSTL *and, just behind them,* NATTER *also
leave for the court.* OTTO *and* GENIA *remain behind.*)

GENIA: Do you believe it?

OTTO: This absurd nonsense about a duel? Of course not.

GENIA: But there could be something behind it . . . In a word,
that I – was *Korsakow*'s mistress, too.

OTTO: No. I don't believe it.

GENIA: Why not? Because I deny it? That's no reason. In your
place . . . I'd believe it.
(*She makes as if to go to the court.*)

OTTO: I don't believe it, Genia. I swear to you, Genia, I don't

believe it. Why are we talking about it? Please don't go!
Please! – who knows if we'll have another moment alone
together. First thing tomorrow I've got to go to town, and
I'm going to Polla by the night train.

GENIA: (*Looking at him*) Is it tomorrow. . . ?

OTTO: How will I be able to let you know what's happening to
me?

GENIA: You can write. My letters aren't opened. And if you
wanted to be especially careful, then simply write to me just
as you are talking to me now – as to an old friend.

OTTO: I couldn't do that. Don't ask it of me.

GENIA: Then – don't write at all.

OTTO: Genia . . .

GENIA: Wouldn't that be the most sensible thing? After all, we
won't be seeing each other again.

OTTO: Genia! I'll be back in three years.

GENIA: (*Smiling*) In three years!

OTTO: And how am I to live . . . without you?

GENIA: You'll live. It was lovely. Let's call it a day. Pleasant
journey, Otto, and good luck for the future.

OTTO: Will you remember me, Genia?

GENIA: Oh, yes. And I'll forget you too.

OTTO: Do you enjoy hurting me?

GENIA: Why do you think me better than I am? I'm not better
than other people. Haven't you noticed? I lie, I'm a
hypocrite. I act out this farce for everybody – for Mr Natter
and for Mrs Wahl . . . for your mother just as for my own
housemaid. I act the part of a respectable married woman –
and at night leave my window open for my lover. I write
and tell my son he can stay longer with his friends, to my
darling boy I write that . . . just so that he won't spoil my
fun – and then I write to tell my husband that Joey absolute
insists on staying on in England so that *he* doesn't hurry
back either. And when he comes back today and shakes
hands with you, I'll be standing by with a smile on my face
and probably enjoying my cleverness. Do you find all that

particularly attractive? Do you think – there's a person you can trust – ? Believe me, Otto, I'm just like the others.

(FRIEDRICH *appears on the balcony, speaking as he appears.*)

FRIEDRICH: Friends, Romans and countrymen! Hello there. I'm just changing.

GENIA: (*Not alarmed*) Friedrich!

OTTO: Good evening, Mr Hofreiter.

FRIEDRICH: Hello there, Otto.

GENIA: (*Cheerfully*) When did you get back?

FRIEDRICH: Got here ten minutes ago. (*To* OTTO) I'm pleased to find you are still here. I was afraid you'd already be in Polla . . . or even on the high seas.

OTTO: I'm leaving tomorrow, Mr Hofreiter.

FRIEDRICH: So . . . tomorrow? Well, I'll be right down.

(*He leaves the balcony.* OTTO *and* GENIA *move across. The following is very quick.*)

OTTO: You can't stay here.

GENIA: Be reasonable, Otto.

OTTO: I know it now. You weren't made for deceit. I was, perhaps, but not you. You would give yourself away. Or just blurt it out deliberately.

GENIA: Possibly.

OTTO: (*Suddenly deciding*) I'm going to tell him.

GENIA: For heaven's sake!

OTTO: Yes – it's the only thing to do – anything else would be cowardly –

GENIA: I'll tell him as soon as you've gone. Tomorrow.

OTTO: And what will happen?

GENIA: Nothing, probably. I don't want you to come here again, ever. Promise me . . . never . . . not even in three years . . . never . . .

OTTO: (*Understanding*) You love him – you still love him!

(MRS WAHL, NATTER, ADELE, STANZIDES *and* GUSTL *come from the court.* ERNA *and* PAUL *carry on playing.* FRIEDRICH *meets them amid greetings and rejoicing.*)

FRIEDRICH: Hello there, Genia.

(*Kisses her on the forehead. To* MRS WAHL, *who refuses him her hand*) Come, come, Mama Wahl, are you still cross with me?

MRS WAHL: I'm not speaking to you. And I'm not speaking to Dr Mauer either.

FRIEDRICH: We'll have to see about that.

GENIA: He hasn't shown up at all yet.

FRIEDRICH: Really? – I hope he'll come today. I've written him a note. Well, Paul and Erna naturally refuse to be put off their game.

GENIA: Tell me, when did you arrive in Vienna?

FRIEDRICH: Last night. Yes – I would very much have liked to come out here earlier. But unfortunately it was quite impossible.

GENIA: We gave a luncheon party in your honour.

GUSTL: It was a great success none the less.

FRIEDRICH: Indeed. . . ? Well I'll have a cup of black coffee anyway.

(*He sits and lights a cigarette.*)

NATTER: You stayed away longer than you intended, my dear Hofreiter?

FRIEDRICH: Yes. (*He looks sharply at* NATTER.) Yes. Aren't those your children leaping about in the field over there?

ADELE: I thought young Joey would be here by now.

(STANZIDES *and* MRS WAHL *have meanwhile moved upstage.*)

FRIEDRICH: Well, when is he coming? Getting himself invited to English country houses . . .

(ERNA *and* PAUL *come from the court.*)

PAUL: My compliments, Mr Hofreiter.

FRIEDRICH: Paul! How is everything?

PAUL: I can't get my service right.

ERNA: Good evening, Friedrich.

(*They shake hands.*)

FRIEDRICH: And did you continue to have a pleasant time at Lake Vols?

ERNA: Yes – imagine it – very pleasant, even without you.

Incidentally, that really wasn't very nice of you to disappear
so suddenly. Oh yes, by the way, thank you for your
postcards . . . You certainly had a lovely trip.

FRIEDRICH: Your fame has reached the papers today, Erna.

MRS WAHL: We've already seen it.

FRIEDRICH: So, you've already – you mean this newspaper has
found its way here too? – An interesting rag – isn't it?
(*Pause. He is amused by the others' embarrassment.*)
Oh, where's Otto? –
(OTTO *is standing somewhat aside.*)
. . . I have to pass on remembrances – or more precisely,
lack of remembrances – but I've spoken to your father.

OTTO: Your wife told me.

FRIEDRICH: It's a shame you're going away tomorrow. Your
father wanted to come to Vienna for a few days. That you
should sail off into the blue, without seeing him, it doesn't
seem right . . . does it?

OTTO: Perhaps – but now it's too late.
(PAUL, *who has been standing with* ERNA *and* MRS WAHL,
comes forward.)

PAUL: Well then, Lieutenant, our singles match, if you don't
mind. I quite understand if none of you want to watch.

OTTO: I'll go and get changed.

PAUL: You see, we're only playing singles today. You are not
exempt, Mr Hofreiter; the Lieutenant is leaving tomorrow
and so the position must be settled once and for all.

FRIEDRICH: I am at your disposal. When I've finished my coffee.
(NATTER, STANZIDES, GENIA – *after* FRIEDRICH's *first
words to* OTTO *about* DR VON AIGNER – *and* GUSTL, *have
already moved somewhat apart and are now followed by* PAUL,
ADELE *and* OTTO. *This leaves* ERNA *and* FRIEDRICH. ERNA
remains standing behind his chair.)
Oh Erna . . .
(*He remains seated.*)

ERNA: I'm so glad to have you back.

FRIEDRICH: Really?

(*He kisses her hand over the back of the chair.*)

So am I.

ERNA: And now I'd like to know your real reason for going away.

FRIEDRICH: You are a funny girl. I told you. If I'd stayed, in a few days – oh God, on the same day – the whole hotel would have known about us. You know why . . . the sinner's halo, you called it.

ERNA: Lover's.

FRIEDRICH: Exactly! We'd done enough to earn it.

ERNA: And what if someone *had* noticed?

FRIEDRICH: Dear girl . . . that's not something to be given away to the world. And the less you think of the world, the less you should give it away. You should be grateful to me for not compromising your reputation. Later you would have come to blame me for it.

ERNA: Later? Oh, I see . . . But I'll never marry, Friedrich.

FRIEDRICH: Don't speak too soon, my darling. You should never try to look into the future. Not even into the next moment. Believe me.

ERNA: And do you think that if I ever loved anyone after you, I'd be able to keep silent about us?

FRIEDRICH: Of course you could. And you would be right to.

ERNA: Another man might think differently – a better man.

FRIEDRICH: You think so?

(*He stands up.*)

ERNA: What's the matter with you? Why are you so nervous? Are you expecting somebody?

FRIEDRICH: Yes, Mauer.

ERNA: Dr Mauer? What do you want from him?

FRIEDRICH: A business matter.

ERNA: He's a doctor of medicine.

FRIEDRICH: He's also a friend.

ERNA: Do you think he still is?

FRIEDRICH: Yes. Friendship is above incident. These things don't depend on . . . events. He could shoot me dead and it would still be his friend he'd shot.

ERNA: What is this business that's so important?

FRIEDRICH: Come on, my sweetheart! A wife couldn't be more inquisitive. Anyway, it's just boring business.

ERNA: It seems to make you very nervous.

FRIEDRICH: Do I give that impression? Far from it. It's probably that I'm just rather short of sleep. I was keeping a vigil under someone's window.

ERNA: Last night?

FRIEDRICH: Yes, last night. Why are you so surprised? I told you one evening . . . I suddenly understand all those things – serenades . . . duels . . . suicide . . .

ERNA: I don't understand you. Who were you . . . who's window. . . ?

FRIEDRICH: Well, yours of course.

ERNA: Mine? What a romancer you are –

FRIEDRICH: You don't believe me? Then listen. Yesterday evening I did come on out here. Straight after arriving in Vienna. It was almost midnight when I was beneath your window. You still had a light burning. I saw your shadow glide past the curtains. If your room had been on the ground floor . . . who knows . . .

ERNA: And then?

FRIEDRICH: And then I went away again. Back to town. I had been near you. That's all I wanted.

ERNA: You were beneath my windows! . . . Friedrich!

FRIEDRICH: Would I tell you if it weren't true? . . .

ERNA: You were underneath my window! . . . My lover.

FRIEDRICH: Ssh . . . ssh . . .

(FRIEDRICH *moves to the door of the house.* MAUER *comes out.*)

MAUER: Hello, Friedrich. Good evening, Miss Erna.

FRIEDRICH: I'm glad to see you, Mauer.

ERNA: (*Calmly*) Good evening, Doctor.

MAUER: (*Quite collected*) Have you been back long, Miss Erna?

ERNA: Just for two days . . . (*To* FRIEDRICH) You want to speak to the doctor, I'll see you later.

(*She goes towards the tennis court.*)

MAUER: You wrote to me, so here I am.

FRIEDRICH: It was good of you to come. I hope I'm not keeping you from anything important.

MAUER: Your note said you needed my advice. I take it you're not feeling well.

FRIEDRICH: (*Looks at him.*) I see! – No, it wasn't the doctor I wanted to see, it was the friend.

MAUER: The friend, I see . . . Well, here I am.

FRIEDRICH: Actually, it's about an absurd rumour which perhaps you've already heard about or read about.

MAUER: That Korsakow died in an American duel? Heard it, to tell you the truth.

FRIEDRICH: Well then, what am I to do?

MAUER: What are you to do? You've got Korsakow's letter to your wife which shows that he had other reasons to kill himself.

FRIEDRICH: What good is that to me . . . I couldn't possibly . . . it would be very bad form . . .

MAUER: All right then . . . just don't worry about it. The rumour will disappear as it came.

FRIEDRICH: Someone opened his mouth to put this libel about. I want to nail him.

MAUER: Whoever it is, you'd have a job to find out.

FRIEDRICH: As far as I'm concerned I've found him. It's Natter.

MAUER: You think so?

FRIEDRICH: It's his revenge . . . After all . . . he knew . . .

MAUER: (*Quickly*) Everything, I'm sure.

FRIEDRICH: Yes – there aren't anything like as many deceived husbands around as their wives like to think.

MAUER: Have you any proof that he planted the rumour?

FRIEDRICH: Proof, no.

MAUER: Then there's nothing you can do.

FRIEDRICH: I could accuse him to his face.

MAUER: Naturally he'd deny it.

FRIEDRICH: Give him a good hiding.

MAUER: That wouldn't help.

FRIEDRICH: Might help my mood.

MAUER: As a means to an end, it would be somewhat disproportionate.

FRIEDRICH: I don't think so. A good mood is very important.

MAUER: I would let the matter drop. With the best will in the world I can't advise you differently – so now I'll say good evening to your wife and then be on my way.

FRIEDRICH: You can damn well do that later! For the moment you'll be kind enough to stay here – All right, I kissed Erna once . . . I don't deny that. A kiss like that in the open air, on a beautiful day, at ten thousand feet, doesn't mean a thing. I'll call it vertigo.

MAUER: Well . . . if that's what you'd call it . . . then everything's all right.

FRIEDRICH: Do you think there are lots of unkissed girls running around the world? It's even been known to happen at sea level! A kiss! – For a chap to think he's too good for a girl . . . just because . . . forgive me, but that's megalomania.

MAUER: You get great pleasure out of lying, don't you?

FRIEDRICH: Enormous – at times. But on this occasion I'm denying myself. And let me tell you something else. Even if there'd been anything more to it . . . more than this kiss . . .

MAUER: I haven't asked you. And I assure you it makes no difference to me how far things have gone between you.

FRIEDRICH: Ah, but it does, my dear Mauer.

MAUER: Oh. . . ?

FRIEDRICH: It might have been better for you if we had become lovers. The affair would have been over and done with. In a way you'd be more secure.

MAUER: I'm beginning to find you amusing.

FRIEDRICH: Well, that's something. Since certainty is unattainable, entertainment value is the only justification for conversation.

MAUER: I'd be able to get the truth from Erna herself.

FRIEDRICH: You think so?

MAUER: I think that lying is the one thing left she is incapable of.

FRIEDRICH: You could be right. And that's worth a thousand times more than so-called respectability. Look at Genia.

MAUER: I beg your pardon?

FRIEDRICH: My wife, Genia. Her affair with Otto.

MAUER: Your wife?

FRIEDRICH: Didn't you know? Well, what have you got to say about that?

MAUER: If it is true . . .

FRIEDRICH: Then it serves me right. I know. But let me tell you that your satisfaction is misplaced – for I'd have to find the affair hurtful, or at least irritating. But that is not the case. On the contrary. It's more like a happy release. I'm no longer the guilty party in this house. I can breathe freely again. It's almost as if she's atoned for Korsakow's death, and indeed in a most rational and painless way. She's begun to close the distance between us, as human beings. We are once more living, as it were, on the same planet.

MAUER: I congratulate you on your poise. Clearly you don't believe a word of it: since one can never know for certain . . .

FRIEDRICH: I could be jumping to conclusions. All I've got to go on is seeing Otto climbing out of my wife's bedroom window at one-thirty in the morning.

MAUER: Which morning?

FRIEDRICH: This morning. I in fact arrived last night, you see.

MAUER: Really? And where were you until half-past one in the morning?

FRIEDRICH: Ha ha . . . You can't think of anything but Erna, can you? Well, just to reassure you, I came out here to Baden on the last train from Vienna; walked here from the station and came, as I sometimes do, through the little gate from the field into the garden. And then to my surprise, I hear voices. I creep nearer and I see a gentleman and a lady sitting under the tree there. Genia and Otto. At midnight, here in the garden. Of course I can't catch what they are saying. I keep my distance. After a few minutes they both get up and disappear into the house. I quickly leave the garden, go up through the back gate again, go around the house and position myself so that I'm bound to see anyone leaving the house by the front gate. No one comes. No one comes for half an hour. The lights in the house go out. I quickly retrace my steps, go round the fence and into the field, where I can keep my eye on Genia's bedroom window. (*Pause.*) It was dark. It was a beautiful night. I lay down on the grass in the shadow of the tree by the fence. And I waited. I waited until half-past one. At half-past one the window opened, a gentleman climbed out, disappeared from my view in the darkness of the garden. I heard the garden gate close, and immediately afterwards the slender figure of Lieutenant Otto von Aigner floated right past me.

MAUER: I hope you're not thinking of making him and Genia pay for it. The only thing for you to do now – the thing that you ought to do – is to make a complete break. It could be done now with very little fuss. You need only go to America a little earlier than you had planned.

FRIEDRICH: Genia's coming to America with me.

MAUER: Oh yes?

FRIEDRICH: Yes.

MAUER: (*Shrugging*) Allow me to take that, for the time being, as the ultimate expression of your self-regard. Now . . . if you'll excuse me, I'll say good evening to your wife.

FRIEDRICH: She'll be so pleased.

(MAUER *goes to the tennis court, passing* NATTER.)

NATTER: (*Entering*) Oh, good evening, Dr Mauer, how are you? Forgive me, dear Hofreiter, I just wanted to ask you . . . as we can't stay any longer, alas . . . if I could come to see you at your office tomorrow. That syndicate has shown up again. They're offering . . .

FRIEDRICH: Business tomorrow, Mr Natter.

NATTER: As you wish.

FRIEDRICH: Today we'll chat.

NATTER: With pleasure.

FRIEDRICH: Tell me, Natter, what do you make of Demeter Stanzides?

NATTER: Stanzides? A nice enough fellow. A bit soft-hearted for a captain in the Hussars. But a decent chap on the whole.

FRIEDRICH: Hasn't he got debts?

NATTER: Not to my knowledge.

FRIEDRICH: Doesn't he mistreat his subordinates?

NATTER: I've never heard anything like that.

FRIEDRICH: Does he perhaps cheat at cards?

NATTER: Do you have reason to think so, Hofreiter?

FRIEDRICH: No. I just wanted to make it easier for you to get something on him later on, when his affair with your wife is over.

(FRIEDRICH *and* NATTER *are standing face to face.*)

NATTER: I'm glad you don't think me a fool, Hofreiter.

FRIEDRICH: No . . . I think you're a . . .

NATTER: I warn you not to call me a scoundrel. I may not find it convenient to settle this business over a game of billiards.

FRIEDRICH: There are other ways.

NATTER: If I had wanted to challenge you . . . I would have had better cause not so long ago.

FRIEDRICH: Why didn't you? A man doesn't change . . . As a young man in uniform you risked your precious life for less than that.

NATTER: For less? For something else.

FRIEDRICH: If it meant so little to you – why do you stay with your wife?

NATTER: So little? To me life without Adele would mean absolutely nothing at all. The fact is I'm hopelessly in love with her. It does happen, Hofreiter. There's nothing I can do about it. You have no idea how many ways I've tried, to break free of my need of her. In vain . . . all in vain . . . I love her despite everything. Ridiculous, isn't it? – But there it is.

FRIEDRICH: And you revenge yourself by inventing ridiculous tales about me?

NATTER: It could be the truth.

FRIEDRICH: God! – Do you really believe that? . . . that I . . . an American duel . . .

NATTER: Prove you didn't.

FRIEDRICH: I could do that – I know the reason for Korsakow's suicide. I happen to know that . . . Oh, what have I come to? Justifying myself to you, you –

NATTER: Careful now.

(PAUL *and* OTTO *enter from the tennis court.*)

OTTO: Time for our singles match now, Mr Hofreiter.

FRIEDRICH: Just coming.

PAUL: *You* see if you can beat him.

(PAUL *and* OTTO *return to the tennis court.*)

FRIEDRICH: I swear to you that you're wrong. I swear to you on . . .

NATTER: On your wife's virtue, perhaps?

FRIEDRICH: Sir –

(*He goes up to* NATTER.)

NATTER: Calm down, we don't want any fuss. I'm not going to brawl with you. But just one word more and . . .

FRIEDRICH: So I am to be at the mercy of you, of someone who . . .

NATTER: Someone who finds life wonderfully amusing . . . dear Hofreiter – and no more than that.

PAUL: (*Returning*) Sorry to interrupt . . .

FRIEDRICH: Yes . . . yes . . . I'm ready – let the position be settled once and for all . . .

NATTER: Once and for all – to the death, perhaps?

FRIEDRICH: Why not?

NATTER: Don't let me keep you.

(MAUER *and* GENIA *come from upstage.*)

FRIEDRICH: (*To* MAUER) No, you simply cannot go. You must

keep him here, Genia – use all your powers of seduction.

(FRIEDRICH, PAUL *and* NATTER *go to the court.*)

GENIA: I'm afraid my powers will prove insufficient.

MAUER: Unfortunately I'm afraid I must go, Gnädige Frau.

GENIA: Am I right in thinking we won't be seeing you here for some time? I don't want to force myself into your confidence. I can guess what is driving you away from us.

MAUER: This time I cannot congratulate you on your perspicacity.

GENIA: I'm sorry to have lost a friend.

MAUER: Now if you'll allow me, Gnädige Frau, I must take my leave.

GENIA: It's not for me to allow you or forbid you, still less as Gnädige Frau!

(MAUER *turns back to* GENIA *and they embrace.*)

Goodbye, dear Doctor! – And . . . please let me give you one piece of advice to go with you – Don't take it too hard. It would be silly for you, who see life at its most truly serious, to take seriously these foolish games. Well, that's all that love affairs are, Doctor, believe me. And once you've accepted that, they're very enjoyable to watch – even to take part in.

MAUER: Once you have accepted that . . .

GENIA: You will too, my friend. And all those silly, overblown words that fill your mind – you'll see how empty they really are. They just blow away.

MAUER: And only the lies remain. Don't they matter either?

GENIA: Lies? Can one have lies in a game? That's called bluff, all part of the fun.

MAUER: A game? Oh yes, if that's how it was played! I assure you, Genia, I would have nothing at all against a world in which love really was in fact nothing but a delightful game . . . But in that case . . . in that case let it be played honestly if you will, let it be rotten with honesty, then perhaps you have a point. But this hole-in-the-corner posturing, this bogus civility between people made wretched by jealousy, cowardice, lust – I find all that sad and horrible – This much-vaunted freedom one finds here lacks conviction. That's why the happiness it seeks eludes it . . . and why its laughter dies in a grin.

GENIA: Oh really, you're going too far. We all make an effort, though of course it doesn't always go as well as we would like. But we do have the best of intentions. Haven't you noticed? Adele Natter visits, I chat to Erna, Friedrich plays his game of tennis with the Lieutenant . . .

MAUER: And why shouldn't he?

GENIA: Oh, Doctor! . . .

MAUER: Yes, I know . . . Tread carefully, Genia.
(*The tennis game is over. The players are gradually coming back.*)

GENIA: Why 'tread carefully'? – Friedrich won't mind. After all, Otto might have killed himself too, if I hadn't . . . Like the other one. And one mustn't drive a young chap to blow his brains out over a trifle like one's own virtue. Friedrich will give me his blessing. Tomorrow when . . . my lover has gone . . . I'll tell him all about it myself.

MAUER: That won't be necessary. He saw the Lieutenant last night . . . at half-past one.
(GENIA *starts, then pulls herself together quickly.* PAUL, STANZIDES, GUSTL, ERNA, ADELE, MRS WAHL, NATTER, OTTO *and* FRIEDRICH *come from the court.*)

GENIA: Well, who won?

PAUL: The old guard lives on. Mr Hofreiter won.

STANZIDES: Pity you didn't see it, ma'am. It was a fine game.

FRIEDRICH: So, Mauer, you stayed after all. That's nice of you!

PAUL: Next it's the game between Miss Erna and Mr Hofreiter.

ERNA: It's already too dark, we'll postpone it till tomorrow.

FRIEDRICH: What a shame that we couldn't have played another game tomorrow, Otto! I didn't really enjoy my victory today.

PAUL: Why ever not? The Lieutenant played very well and you played a blinder.

FRIEDRICH: I don't know. You weren't on top form, Otto. You had one stroke I've never noticed before in your armoury. Such a nervous indecisive stroke as if your mind was elsewhere. Upset to be going, I suppose.

OTTO: Well, when I return in three years, Mr Hofreiter, I hope to be a better match for you.

FRIEDRICH: Yes, if one could be sure we would see each other again! . . . I never look as far ahead . . . Think of all the things that can happen. We are not masters of our fate. Anything might happen to make all prediction useless . . . and all caution.

NATTER: And caution doesn't happen to be one of the Lieutenant's strong points.

OTTO: I'm only too aware of that myself, Mr Natter.

FRIEDRICH: There's no way you could know, Otto, whether or not you're cautious by nature . . . In a profession where so much depends on morale and discipline as in yours, you can't know what your nature really is, don't you think?

MAUER: It's getting late for psychology. (*To* OTTO) Shall we go together?

FRIEDRICH: (*Ignoring this*) I don't doubt for a moment, of course, that you would be ready to lay down your life for king and country, but external pressures play a certain role in that. In the depths of your soul, in the very depths, Otto, you're a coward.
(*Long pause.*)

OTTO: I haven't understood you correctly, have I?

FRIEDRICH: I don't know what you understood. In any case I'll repeat it: you are a coward.
(OTTO *takes a step towards* FRIEDRICH. FRIEDRICH *moves quickly to meet him.*)

OTTO: You will hear from me.

FRIEDRICH: I hope so – (*quietly*) – and soon.
(OTTO *leaves.* PAUL *speaks quietly to* GUSTL *and they follow* OTTO. ERNA *and* GENIA *stand motionless.* MRS WAHL *looks round helplessly and turns to* ADELE.)

NATTER: Well, I think that's everything.

FRIEDRICH: No, don't go yet. (*To* MAUER, *aside*) Mauer, I hope I can count on you.

MAUER: No. I'll have nothing to do with it.

FRIEDRICH: As a doctor, Mauer. You can't deny me that, it's your duty.

MAUER: (*Shrugging*) Very well.

FRIEDRICH: Thank you. Dear Stanzides.

STANZIDES: I am at your disposal.

FRIEDRICH: I thank you. Natter, can I ask you?

NATTER: My dear Hofreiter . . .

FRIEDRICH: (*Pulling* NATTER *downstage*) I think we share the same view of life, don't we? Too funny for words.

NATTER: I've always said so.

FRIEDRICH: This latest joke would have one more twist for me – if you would be my second.

NATTER: Only too pleased – the Lieutenant is bound to be a good shot.

GENIA: (*Suddenly decided, goes to* FRIEDRICH) Friedrich . . .

FRIEDRICH: Later.

GENIA: Now.

FRIEDRICH: (*To the others*) Excuse us.

(FRIEDRICH *moves downstage with* GENIA. MRS WAHL *goes over to* ERNA, *tries to get her to leave.* ERNA *gestures her away and stands by the wall of the house.* MRS WAHL *turns to* ADELE, *who is watching her husband.* NATTER *and* STANZIDES *move upstage.* MAUER *stands by himself.*)

GENIA: What on earth are you doing? How can you . . . ?

FRIEDRICH: Look, don't worry. I won't do much to him, probably nothing at all.

GENIA: Then why? If it had anything at all to do with your feeling for me . . . if it were hate . . . rage . . . jealousy . . . love . . .

FRIEDRICH: That's right – I couldn't give a damn about any of that. But I won't be made to look a fool.

(FRIEDRICH *turns from* GENIA *and follows* NATTER *and*

138

STANZIDES. GENIA *stands downstage motionless.* ERNA
*remains standing by the wall of the house. The two women look
at each other.*)

ACT FIVE

A room in the Hofreiter villa, adjoining the conservatory of Act One. Light and friendly. The french windows leading to the conservatory are open.
GENIA *is in the room, in an agitated state.* ERNA, *hatless, in a summer dress, enters very quickly from the conservatory.*

GENIA: (*Rising, quickly composing herself*) Erna? . . . What's the matter?
ERNA: They aren't back yet? Isn't there any news?
GENIA: How could there be? Get a grip on yourself, Erna. Nothing can happen till this afternoon at the earliest. I should think they're still discussing formalities.
ERNA: (*Looking at her*) Yes, of course. You don't mind my asking. . . ? I know I have no right, but . . .
GENIA: You have as much right to tremble for someone as I have.
ERNA: I'm not trembling, Mrs Hofreiter. I never tremble. I simply wanted to ask if you had seen your husband today?
GENIA: My husband went into town yesterday evening. Arranging various matters with his lawyer, by all accounts. That's quite usual, even if it is superfluous. He will settle his affairs. Perhaps even burn some letters and papers. In brief, behave just as if it were a deadly serious business instead of this charade of a foolish vanity defending a travestied honour – which is what we all know it to be.
ERNA: I'm not convinced of that, Frau Genia.
GENIA: I am. Come on, Erna, let's go into the garden, it's such a lovely day. Let's have a chat. You haven't told me anything about your travels yet. You had an interesting time . . . at Lake Vols . . .
ERNA: Is it possible that you can mock me at such a time, Genia?

GENIA: I'm not mocking you. It's the last thing I . . . You love him
very much – don't you. . . ?! Well, it's only to be expected –
There's nothing like the first time. Or doesn't even that mean
anything nowadays? You must tell me about that, Erna.
When I was your age, one still took certain things terribly
seriously. Now, I don't know where I am any more.
(KATHI *enters with a telegram and then leaves.*)
(*Opening it quickly*) Joey's arriving at midday. It'll be lovely
to see him again. Come on, why don't we go into the
garden, Erna?

ERNA: Genia! At five o'clock this morning I saw Gustl leave.
The duel took place at six. While we're talking it's all long
since been over.
(*Pause.*)

GENIA: So, everything is over . . . Now nothing can be
changed, isn't that so? Then they'll all be sitting down
together at the convent, under the shade of a tree and
toasting the reconciliation . . . Erna, do you think they'll be
drinking our health? Why not? Perhaps they'll turn up here
together arm-in-arm. Yes . . . we should go and meet
them . . .
(MRS VON AIGNER *is seen approaching from the conservatory.*)

ERNA: It's Otto's mother.

GENIA: (*Starts.*) What. . . ?

ERNA: She's walking quite calmly. She doesn't know anything.

GENIA: What's she doing here so early?

ERNA: She certainly doesn't know anything. She's quite
unconcerned. Why should she know, anyway? Get hold of
yourself, Frau Genia!

MRS VON AIGNER: (*Entering*) Good morning.

ERNA: Good morning, ma'am.

GENIA: It's you, Mrs von Aigner. Ah . . .
(*She rises.*)

ERNA: Goodbye, then . . .

MRS VON AIGNER: You're going? I hope I'm not driving you
away?

ERNA: Not at all, ma'am. I had just taken my leave. Goodbye, Frau Genia.

GENIA: (*With tremendous self-control*) I'm delighted to see you again, Mrs von Aigner. We missed you yesterday.

MRS VON AIGNER: There were so many of you. I don't like a large crowd. Today I'm here all the earlier, as you see, Mrs Hofreiter.

GENIA: Is it so early? Friedrich went into town hours ago. You know of course, Mrs von Aigner, that he got back yesterday.

MRS VON AIGNER: Of course I know. (*Smiling*) Otto conveyed Mr Hofreiter's respects to me last evening.

GENIA: I see. Your son is leaving you today. . . ?

MRS VON AIGNER: My son has in fact already left. He caught the last train yesterday. And this evening he's travelling to Polla.

GENIA: This evening, is it? Ah!

MRS VON AIGNER: Was I really the first to tell you that?

GENIA: No, I did know.

MRS VON AIGNER: Can you imagine, Mrs Hofreiter, how I felt this morning as I sat down to breakfast in my summerhouse, once again quite alone. My little house is suddenly so empty . . . I had become unused to that. I suppose I've been really spoiled for quite some while – in spite of everything. I wanted to go for a walk . . . a walk by myself in the woods. And now I'm here. I don't know how that happened. Something must have directed my steps.

(*She looks at* GENIA *for a long moment.*)

GENIA: (*Returning her look*) Thank you.

MRS VON AIGNER: You mustn't thank me. I had the choice of being very angry with you – or of being very fond of you. And when I left home I was still far from decided. Because in these last few days – now that he's gone I can tell you, I suppose, Genia – I have sometimes really been afraid . . .

GENIA: Afraid – ?

MRS VON AIGNER: I do know my son . . . And I've seen how much he's suffered recently. He wasn't made at all . . . for deceit . . . I was . . . afraid for him . . . You meant so much